Table of Contents

Table of Contents

Name: _____

Identifying the Parts of a Sentence

The **subject** tells who or what the sentence is about. The subject is always a noun or pronoun. A **noun** is a word that names a person, place or thing. A **pronoun** is a word that takes the place of a noun.

Example:

The handsome **boy** danced yesterday.
Boy is the subject. The sentence is about the boy.

A verb tells what something does or that something exists.

Example:

The handsome boy **danced** yesterday.
Danced is the verb. It shows action.

An adverb tells when, where or how something happened.

Example:

The handsome boy danced **yesterday**.
Yesterday is an adverb. It tells when the boy danced.

An adjective describes a noun.

Example:

The **handsome** boy danced yesterday.

Handsome is an adjective. It describes the noun **boy**.

Directions: Write **N** for noun, **V** for verb, **ADJ** for adjective or **ADV** for adverb for the bold word in each sentence.

_____ 1. She is an **excellent** singer.

_____ 2. The huge black **horse** easily won the race.

_____ 3. The **red-haired** girl was shy.

_____ 4. Joshua **quickly** finished his homework and went out to play.

_____ 5. **Carrots** are my least favorite vegetable.

_____ 6. Why should **I** always have to take out the trash?

_____ 7. That girl **ran** like the wind!

_____ 8. Elizabeth **told** her sister to pick her up at noon.

_____ 9. He was glad he had a **warm** coat to wear.

_____ 10. I live **nearby**.

Name: _____

Nouns

A noun names a person, place or thing.

Examples:

> **person** — sister, uncle, boy, woman
> **place** — building, city, park, street
> **thing** — workbook, cat, candle, bed

Directions: Circle the nouns in each sentence. The first one has been done for you.

1. The (dog) ran into the (street.)

2. Please take this book to the librarian.

3. The red apples are in the kitchen.

4. That scarf belongs to the bus driver.

5. Get some blue paper from the office to make a card.

6. Look at the parachute!

7. Autumn leaves are beautiful.

8. The lion roared loudly at the visitors.

Directions: Write the nouns you circled in the correct group.

Persons	Places	Things	
librarian	street	dog	

Name: _____

Nouns

Directions: Write nouns that name persons.

1. Could you please give this report to my _____?

2. The _____ works many long hours to plant crops.

3. I had to help my little _____ when he wrecked his bike yesterday.

Directions: Write nouns that name places.

4. I always keep my library books on top of the _____ so I can find them.

5. We enjoyed watching the kites flying high in the _____ .

6. Dad built a nice fire in the _____ to keep us warm.

Directions: Write nouns that name things.

7. The little _____ purred softly as I held it.

8. Wouldn't you think a _____ would get tired of carrying its house around all day?

9. The _____ scurried into its hole with the piece of cheese.

10. I can tell by the writing that this _____ is mine.

11. Look at the _____ I made in art.

12. His _____ blew away because of the strong wind.

Name: _____

Proper Nouns

Proper nouns name specific persons, places or things.

Examples:

> **person** — Ms. Steiner, Judge Jones, Lt. Raydon
>
> **place** — Crestview School, California, China
>
> **thing** — Declaration of Independence, Encyclopedia Britannica

Directions: Circle the proper noun in each sentence. Write person, place or thing in the blank. The first one has been done for you.

1. I returned the overdue book to the (Ashland Public Library.)

   <u>Ashland Public Library</u>   <u>place</u>

2. Our new principal is Mrs. Denes.

   _____   _____

3. We enjoyed shopping at Brookland Mall.

   _____   _____

4. Did you finish your report on *Charlotte's Web*?

   _____   _____

5. The new student in our class lives on Reed Road.

   _____   _____

6. Mr. Wilkes said he likes his new job.

   _____   _____

7. How do you get to Millsboro from here?

   _____   _____

Charlotte's Web

Proper Nouns in Sentences

Directions: Choose the proper noun from the box to complete each sentence. Then write person, place or thing to describe the type of proper noun.

Michael Jordan	Washington Monument	Empire State Building
Titanic	Grayson Avenue School	Mark McGwire	Fruity-Juice

1. The _____ used to be the tallest building in the United States.

   _____

2. There was a movie made about the _____ , one of the largest ocean liners built.

   _____

3. _____ hit a record number of home runs during the regular season in 1998.

   _____

4. Would you trade this basketball card for your _____ card? He is my favorite basketball player!

   _____

5. I can't wait for lunch! Mom packed some _____ for me to drink.

   _____

6. _____ is my new school. All the teachers there are very friendly.

   _____

Proper Nouns: Capitalization

Proper nouns always begin with a capital letter.

Examples:

> Monday
>
> Texas
>
> Karen
>
> Mr. Logan
>
> Hamburger Avenue
>
> Rover

Directions: Cross out the lower-case letters at the beginning of the proper nouns. Write capital letters above them. The first one has been done for you

1. My teddy bear's name is ~~c~~ocoa. *(C)*

2. ms. bernhard does an excellent job at crestview elementary school.

3. emily, elizabeth and megan live on main street.

4. I am sure our teacher said the book report is due on monday.

5. I believe you can find lake street if you turn left at the next light.

6. Will your family be able join our family for dinner at burger barn?

7. The weather forecasters think the storm will hit the coast of louisiana friday afternoon.

8. My family went to washington, d.c. this summer.

9. Remember, we don't have school on tuesday because of the teachers' meeting.

10. Who do you think will win the game, the cougars or the arrows?

Name: _____

Pronouns

A **pronoun** is a word that takes the place of a noun in a sentence.

Examples:

I, my, mine, me
we, our, ours, us
you, your, yours
he, his, him
she, her, hers
it, its
they, their, theirs, them

Directions: Underline the pronouns in each sentence.

1. Bring them to us as soon as you are finished.

2. She has been my best friend for many years.

3. They should be here soon.

4. We enjoyed our trip to the Mustard Museum.

5. Would you be able to help us with the project on Saturday?

6. Our homeroom teacher will not be here tomorrow.

7. My uncle said that he will be leaving soon for Australia.

8. Hurry! Could you please open the door for him?

9. She dropped her gloves when she got off the bus.

10. I can't figure out who the mystery writer is today.

Nouns and Pronouns

To make a story or report more interesting, pronouns can be substituted for "overused" nouns.

Example:

Mother made the beds. Then Mother started the laundry.

The noun **Mother** is used in both sentences. The pronoun **she** could be used in place of **Mother** the second time to make the second sentence more interesting.

Directions: Cross out nouns when they appear a second and/or third time. Write a pronoun that could be used instead. The first one has been done for you.

__we__ 1. My friends and I like to go ice skating in the winter. ~~My friends and I~~ usually fall down a lot, but ~~my friends and I~~ have fun!

_____ 2. All the children in the fourth-grade class next to us must have been having a party. All the children were very loud. All the children were happy it was Friday.

_____ 3. I try to help my father with work around the house on the weekends. My father works many hours during the week and would not be able to get everything done.

_____ 4. Can I share my birthday treat with the secretary and the principal? The secretary and the principal could probably use a snack right now!

_____ 5. I know Mr. Jones needs a copy of this history report. Please take it to Mr. Jones when you finish.

Name: _____

Nouns and Pronouns

Directions: Cross out nouns when they appear a second and/or third time. Write a pronoun that could be used instead.

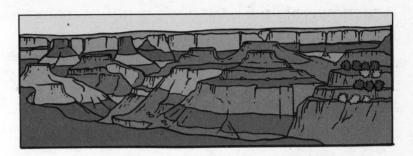

_____ 1. The merry-go-round is one of my favorite rides at the county fair. I ride the merry-go-round so many times that I sometimes get sick.

_____ 2. My parents and I are planning a 2-week vacation next year. My parents and I will be driving across the country to see the Grand Canyon. My parents and I hope to have a great time.

_____ 3. The new art teacher brought many ideas from the city school where the art teacher worked before.

_____ 4. Green beans, corn and potatoes are my favorite vegetables. I could eat green beans, corn and potatoes for every meal. I especially like green beans, corn and potatoes in stew.

_____ 5. I think I left my pen in the library when I was looking up reference materials earlier today. Did you find my pen when you cleaned?

_____ 6. My grandmother makes very good apple pie. My grandmother said I could learn how to make one the next time we visit.

_____ 7. My brothers and I could take care of your pets while you are away if you show my brothers and me what you want done.

Name: _____

Pronoun Referents

A **pronoun referent** is the noun or nouns a pronoun refers to.

Example:

Green beans, corn and potatoes are my favorite vegetables. I could eat them for every meal.

The pronoun **them** refers to the nouns green beans, corn and potatoes.

Directions: Find the pronoun in each sentence, and write it in the blank below. Underline the word the pronoun refers to. The first one has been done for you.

1. <u>The fruit trees</u> look so beautiful in the spring when they are covered with blossoms.

   _____they_____

2. Tori is a high school cheerleader. She spends many hours at practice.

   _____

3. The football must have been slippery because of the rain. The quarterback could not hold on to it.

   _____

4. Aunt Donna needs a babysitter for her three year old tonight.

   _____

5. The art projects are on the table. Could you please put them on the top shelf along the wall?

   _____

Pronoun Referents

Directions: Find the pronoun in each sentence, and write it in the blank below. Underline the word the pronoun refers to.

1. Did Aaron see the movie *Titanic*? Jay thought it was a very good movie.

   _____

2. Maysie can help you with the spelling words now, Tasha.

   _____

3. The new tennis coach said to call him after 6:00 tonight.

   _____

4. Jim, John and Jason called to say they would be later than planned.

   _____

5. Mrs. Burns enjoyed the cake her class had for the surprise party.

   _____

6. The children are waiting outside. Ask Josh to take the pinwheels out to them.

   _____

7. Mrs. Taylor said to go on ahead because she will be late.

   _____

8. The whole team must sit on the bus until the driver gives us permission to get off.

   _____

9. Dad said the umbrella did a poor job of keeping the rain off him.

   _____

10. The umbrella was blowing around too much. That's probably why it didn't do a good job.

    _____

Pronoun Referents

Directions: Read each sentence carefully. Draw a line to connect each sentence to the correct pronoun.

1. All the teachers in our building said _____ could use a day off!   him

2. The whole cast spent a lot of time in rehearsals for the school play. _____ should go very well.   it

3. My Uncle Mike is driving around in a very old car. I know _____ would like to buy a new one.   they

4. Mr. Barker is having some trouble programming that VCR. Can you help _____ ?   she

5. There are too many books on the shelf. I know I can't fit all of _____ into this small box.   them

6. Ms. Hart slipped on the bleachers at the football game. That's why _____ is using crutches.   he

Subjects and Predicates

The **subject** tells who or what the sentence is about. The **predicate** tells what the subject does, did, is doing or will do. A complete sentence must have a subject and a predicate.

Examples:

Subject	Predicate
Sharon	writes to her grandmother every week.
The horse	ran around the track quickly.
My mom's car	is bright green.
Denise	will be here after lunch.

Directions: Circle the subject of each sentence. Underline the predicate.

1. My sister is a very happy person.

2. I wish we had more holidays in the year.

3. Laura is one of the nicest girls in our class.

4. John is fun to have as a friend.

5. The rain nearly ruined our picnic!

6. My birthday present was exactly what I wanted.

7. Your bicycle is parked beside my skateboard.

8. The printer will need to be filled with paper before you use it.

9. Six dogs chased my cat home yesterday!

10. Anthony likes to read anything he can get his hands on.

11. Twelve students signed up for the dance committee.

12. Your teacher seems to be a reasonable person.

Name:

Changing the Subject

Directions: Circle the subject of each sentence. Change the subject to make a new sentence. The word or words you add must make sense with the rest of the sentence. The first one has been done for you.

1. (Twelve students) signed up for the student council elections.

   <u>Only one person in my class signed up for the student council elections.</u>

2. Our whole family went to the science museum last week.

   _____

   _____

3. The funny story made us laugh.

   _____

   _____

4. The brightly colored kites drifted lazily across the sky.

   _____

   _____

5. My little brother and sister spent the whole day at the amusement park.

   _____

   _____

6. The tiny sparrow made a tapping sound at my window.

   _____

   _____

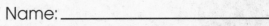

Changing the Predicate

Directions: Circle the predicate in each sentence. Change the predicate to make a new sentence. The words you add must make sense with the rest of the sentence. The first one has been done for you.

1. Twelve students (signed up for the student council elections.)

   <u>Twelve students were absent from my class today!</u>

2. Our whole family went to the science museum last week.

   _____

   _____

3. The funny story made us laugh.

   _____

   _____

4. The brightly colored kites drifted lazily across the sky.

   _____

   _____

5. My little brother and sister spent the whole day at the amusement park.

   _____

   _____

6. The tiny sparrow made a tapping sound at my window.

   _____

   _____

Name: _____

Subjects and Predicates

Directions: Write subjects to complete the following sentences.

1. _____ went to school last Wednesday.

2. _____ did not understand the joke.

3. _____ barked so loudly that no one could sleep a wink.

4. _____ felt unhappy when the ball game was rained out.

5. _____ wonder what happened at the end of the book.

6. _____ jumped for joy when she won the contest.

Directions: Write predicates to complete the following sentences.

7. Everyone _____.

8. Dogs _____.

9. I _____.

10. Justin _____.

11. Jokes _____.

12. Twelve people _____.

Name: _____

Subjects and Predicates

A **sentence** is a group of words that expresses a complete thought. It must have at least one subject and one verb.

Examples:

    Sentence: John felt tired and went to bed early.

    Not a sentence: Went to bed early.

Directions: Write **S** if the group of words is a complete sentence. Write **NS** if the group of words is not a sentence.

_____ 1. Which one of you?

_____ 2. We're happy for the family.

_____ 3. We enjoyed the program very much.

_____ 4. Felt left out and lonely afterwards.

_____ 5. Everyone said it was the best party ever!

_____ 6. No one knows better than I what the problem is.

_____ 7. Seventeen of us!

_____ 8. Quickly before they.

_____ 9. Squirrels are lively animals.

_____ 10. Not many people believe it really happened.

_____ 11. Certainly, we enjoyed ourselves.

_____ 12. Tuned her out.

Subjects and Predicates

Directions: On the previous page, some of the groups of words are not sentences. Rewrite them to make complete sentences.

1. _____

_____

2. _____

_____

3. _____

_____

4. _____

_____

5. _____

_____

Name: _____

Compound Subjects

A **compound subject** is a subject with two parts joined by the word **and** or another conjunction. Compound subjects share the same predicate.

Example:

Her shoes were covered with mud. Her ankles were covered with mud, too.

Compound subject: Her shoes and ankles were covered with mud.

The predicate in both sentences is **were covered with mud**.

Directions: Combine each pair of sentences into one sentence with a compound subject.

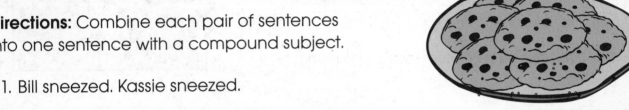

1. Bill sneezed. Kassie sneezed.

_____

2. Kristin made cookies. Joey made cookies.

_____

3. Fruit flies are insects. Ladybugs are insects.

_____

4. The girls are planning a dance. The boys are planning a dance.

_____

5. Our dog ran after the ducks. Our cat ran after the ducks.

_____

6. Joshua got lost in the parking lot. Daniel got lost in the parking lot.

_____

Name: _____

Compound Subjects

If sentences do not share the same predicate, they cannot be combined to write a sentence with a compound subject.

Example: Mary laughed at the story.
Tanya laughed at the television show.

Directions: Combine the pairs of sentences that share the same predicate. Write new sentences with compound subjects.

1. Pete loves swimming. Jake loves swimming.

_____

2. A bee stung Elizabeth. A hornet stung Elizabeth.

_____

3. Sharon is smiling. Susan is frowning.

_____

4. The boys have great suntans. The girls have great suntans.

_____

5. Six squirrels chased the kitten. Ten dogs chased the kitten.

_____

6. The trees were covered with insects. The roads were covered with ice.

_____

Compound Predicates

A **compound predicate** is a predicate with two parts joined by the word **and** or another conjunction. Compound predicates share the same subject.

Example: The baby grabbed the ball. The baby threw the ball.

      Compound predicate: The baby grabbed the ball and threw it. The subject in both sentences is **the baby**.

Directions: Combine each pair of sentences into one sentence to make a compound predicate.

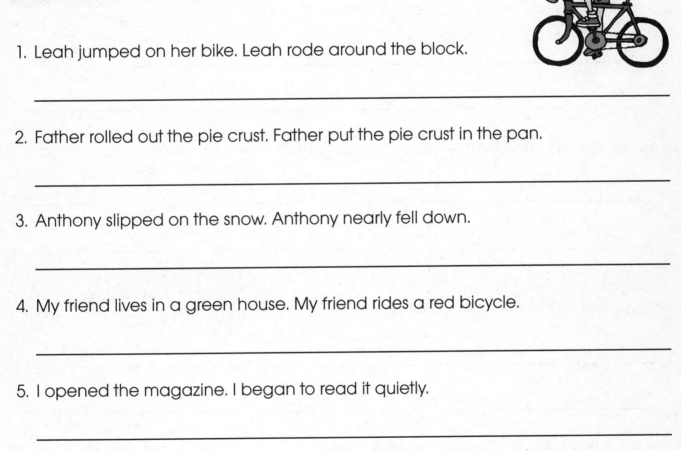

1. Leah jumped on her bike. Leah rode around the block.

_____

2. Father rolled out the pie crust. Father put the pie crust in the pan.

_____

3. Anthony slipped on the snow. Anthony nearly fell down.

_____

4. My friend lives in a green house. My friend rides a red bicycle.

_____

5. I opened the magazine. I began to read it quietly.

_____

6. My father bought a new plaid shirt. My father wore his new red tie.

_____

Name: _____

Compound Predicates

Directions: Combine the pairs of sentences that share the same subject. Write new sentences with compound predicates.

1. Jenny picked a bouquet of flowers. Jenny put the flowers in a vase.

   _____

   _____

2. I really enjoy ice cream. She really enjoys ice cream.

   _____

   _____

3. Everyone had a great time at the pep rally. Then everyone went out for a pizza.

   _____

   _____

4. Cassandra built a model airplane.
   She painted the airplane bright yellow.

   _____

   _____

5. Her brother was really a hard person to get to know. Her sister was very shy, too.

   _____

   _____

Review

Directions: Circle the subjects.

1. Everyone felt the day had been a great success.

2. Christina and Andrea were both happy to take the day off.

3. No one really understood why he was crying.

4. Mr. Winston, Ms. Fuller and Ms. Landers took us on a field trip.

Directions: Underline the predicates.

5. Who can tell what will happen tomorrow?

6. Mark was a carpenter by trade and a talented painter, too.

7. The animals yelped and whined in their cages.

8. Airplane rides made her feel sick to her stomach.

Directions: Combine the sentences to make one sentence with a compound subject.

9. Elizabeth ate everything in sight. George ate everything in sight.

_____

10. Wishing something will happen won't make it so. Dreaming something will happen won't make it so.

_____

Directions: Combine the sentences to make one sentence with a compound predicate.

11. I jumped for joy. I hugged all my friends.

_____

12. She ran around the track before the race. She warmed up before the race.

_____

Name: _____

Intransitive Verbs

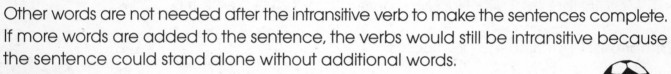

An **intransitive verb** is a verb that can stand alone in the predicate because its meaning is complete.

Examples:

> He **works**.
> They **sleep**.
> The dog **ran**.

Other words are not needed after the intransitive verb to make the sentences complete. If more words are added to the sentence, the verbs would still be intransitive because the sentence could stand alone without additional words.

Example:

> The noisy concert ended early.
> **Ended** is still an intransitive verb in this sentence.

Directions: Underline the intransitive verb in each sentence.

1. The soccer ball bounced out of bounds.

2. Many autumn leaves fell overnight.

3. Our teacher helped at the band concert yesterday.

4. The small, brown puppy whimpered all night.

5. The school band marched across the field.

6. The cat scratched at the door until dark.

7. The fireworks boomed for hours.

8. The school bus arrived late.

9. A few children cried for their mothers.

10. That feather tickles!

11. Grandfather Wade's barn burned last night.

12. The car tires squealed loudly.

13. The audience laughed at the comedian's jokes.

14. The artist painted in the loft studio.

Name: _____

Intransitive Verbs

Directions: Write an intransitive verb after each subject to make a simple sentence.

1. He _____ .

2. Last Wednesday, I _____ .

3. Every February, they _____ .

4. Two summers ago, we _____ .

5. Few people _____ .

6. Several of us _____ .

7. The whole class _____ .

8. No one _____ .

9. Sixteen dogs _____ .

10. A harsh rain _____ .

11. The pony _____ .

12. Two dozen donuts _____ .

Name: _____

Transitive Verbs

A **transitive verb** needs a direct object to complete its meaning. A **direct object** is the word or words that come after a transitive verb to complete its meaning.

Examples:

Tim **is** taking dance lessons.

He **did** a dance.

The dance **was** a gig.

Is, **did** and **was** are transitive verbs. They must have one or more words after them to complete their meanings.

Example:

The bird **found its nest**.

The words **its nest** are needed after the transitive verb **found** to make the sentence complete.

Directions: Underline the transitive verb in each sentence.

1. The computer made a strange sound.

2. Last night's thunderstorm ruined our sand castles.

3. Aunt Jean raised tomatoes in her garden.

4. Brad accepted the award at the dinner last night.

5. Dad saw us outside his window.

6. The students in Home Economics baked delicious brownies.

7. We had a lot of homework.

8. He will replace the dead battery.

9. Everyone saw the special on television last night.

10. My dog chased the cat.

11. Morgan saw the kites flying high in the sky.

12. We enjoyed the museum trip.

Name: _____

Transitive Verbs

Directions: Add a word or words after the transitive verbs to complete the sentences.

1. Sylvia threw _____ .

2. My teacher crossed _____ .

3. No one polished _____ .

4. Several students tickled _____ .

5. The flood destroyed _____ .

6. The elephant found _____ .

7. Six days ago we saw _____ .

8. My favorite book has _____ .

9. The whole class visited _____ .

10. My father said _____ .

11. No one put _____ .

12. Jessica will repair _____ .

Name: _____

Intransitive and Transitive Verbs

Directions: Write a **T** in the blanks by the sentences that have a transitive verb. Write an **I** in the blanks by the sentences that have an intransitive verb.

_____ 1. The story was a mystery.

_____ 2. The people cheered loudly.

_____ 3. The neighbor's dog barked yesterday.

_____ 4. We missed her birthday completely.

_____ 5. The lion roared.

_____ 6. Together, we sang many songs.

_____ 7. Elizabeth sharpened her pencil.

_____ 8. She visited New York City last summer.

_____ 9. The kitten cried for several hours.

_____ 10. Gina arrived late for school.

_____ 11. Did anyone cry when the mayor left?

_____ 12. The thunder boomed loudly.

Name: _____

Intransitive and Transitive Verbs

Directions: Write a **T** in the blanks by the sentences that have a transitive verb. Write an **I** in the blanks by the sentences that have an intransitive verb.

_____ 1. The whole class saw the video on traffic safety.

_____ 2. The eagle soared through the evening sky.

_____ 3. All the monkeys at the zoo chattered noisily.

_____ 4. We did our homework before supper.

_____ 5. The school chorus sang all the songs without the piano.

_____ 6. Mom drew my portrait last summer.

_____ 7. In gym class, we ran for fifteen minutes!

_____ 8. Soon, it was dark.

_____ 9. The bookmobile finally arrived.

_____ 10. The football game was tied.

_____ 11. The tiny kitten cried all night long.

_____ 12. Father drove the van to work today.

_____ 13. Our principal was at school by 7:00 A.M.

_____ 14. My sister got a haircut yesterday.

Name: _____

Review

Directions: Read the definitions. Then write the correct title on the label of each box, using words from the box.

| transitive verb | subject | compound predicate |
| intransitive verb | predicate | compound subject |

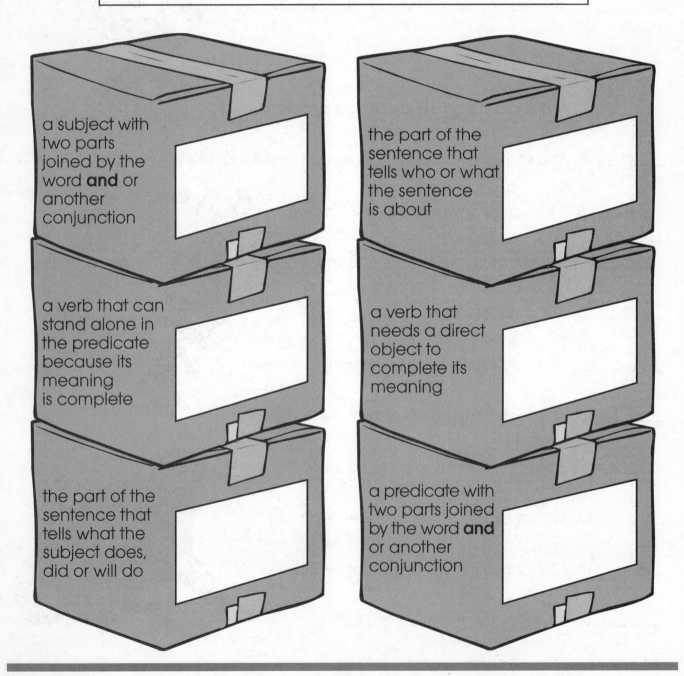

a subject with two parts joined by the word **and** or another conjunction

the part of the sentence that tells who or what the sentence is about

a verb that can stand alone in the predicate because its meaning is complete

a verb that needs a direct object to complete its meaning

the part of the sentence that tells what the subject does, did or will do

a predicate with two parts joined by the word **and** or another conjunction

Verbs: Present, Past and Future Tense

The **present tense** of a verb tells what is happening now.

Examples:

> I **am** happy.
> I **run** fast.

The **past tense** of a verb tells what has already happened.

Examples:

> I **was** happy.
> I **ran** fast.

The **future tense** of a verb refers to what is going to happen. The word **will** usually comes before the future tense of a verb.

Examples:

> I **will be** happy.
> I **will run** fast.

Directions: The sentences below are in the present tense. Rewrite each sentence using the past and future tense of the verb. The first one has been done for you.

1. I think of you as my best friend.
   I thought of you as my best friend.
   I will think of you as my best friend.

2. I hear you coming up the steps.

   _____

   _____

3. I rush every morning to get ready for school.

   _____

   _____

4. I bake brownies every Saturday.

   _____

   _____

Name: _____

Verbs: Present, Past and Future Tense

Directions: Read the following sentences. Write **PRES** if the sentence is in present tense. Write **PAST** if the sentence is in past tense. Write **FUT** if the sentence is in future tense. The first one has been done for you.

__FUT__   1. I will be thrilled to accept the award.

_____   2. Will you go with me to the dentist?

_____   3. I thought he looked familiar!

_____   4. They ate every single slice of pizza.

_____   5. I run myself ragged sometimes.

_____   6. Do you think this project is worthwhile?

_____   7. No one has been able to repair the broken plate.

_____   8. Thoughtful gifts are always appreciated.

_____   9. I like the way he sang!

_____   10. With a voice like that, he will go a long way.

_____   11. It's my fondest hope that they visit soon.

_____   12. I wanted that coat very much.

_____   13. She'll be happy to take your place.

_____   14. Everyone thinks the test will be a breeze.

_____   15. Collecting stamps is her favorite hobby.

Adding "ed" to Make Verbs Past Tense

To make many verbs past tense, add **ed**.

Examples:

cook + ed = cooked   wish + ed = wished   play + ed = played

When a verb ends in a **silent e**, drop the **e** and add **ed**.

Examples:

hope + ed = hoped   hate + ed = hated

When a verb ends in **y** after a consonant, change the **y** to **i** and add **ed**.

Examples:

hurry + ed = hurried   marry + ed = married

When a verb ends in a single consonant after a single short vowel, double the final consonant before adding **ed**.

Examples:

stop + ed = stopped   hop + ed = hopped

Directions: Rewrite the present tense of the verb correctly. The first one has been done for you.

1. call ___called___

2. copy _____

3. frown _____

4. smile _____

5. live _____

6. talk _____

7. name _____

8. list _____

9. spy _____

10. phone _____

11. reply _____

12. top _____

13. clean _____

14. scream _____

15. clap _____

16. mop _____

17. soap _____

18. choke _____

19. scurry _____

20. drop _____

Name: _____

Verbs With "ed"

Directions: All the sentences below need a **verb + ed**. Write a word from the box to complete each sentence.

talked	watched	served	wagged
picked	shared	typed	washed
knocked	laughed	bothered	

1. She _____ on the phone for at least 1 hour.

2. He _____ the vegetables while I prepared the broth for the soup.

3. We never _____ as hard as we did at that clown!

4. Each boy in the class _____ a story about what he had done over the summer.

5. Father _____ the popcorn while Mother put the movie in the VCR.

6. I know that noise _____ you last night.

7. The dog's tail _____ so hard it _____ over the picture on the table.

8. Do you know who _____ the flowers?

9. She carefully _____ her report for health class on the computer.

10. The whole class _____ as the rockets shot up into the sky.

Irregular Verbs: Past Tense

Irregular verbs change completely in the past tense. Unlike regular verbs, past-tense forms of irregular verbs are not formed by adding **ed**.

Example: The past tense of **go** is **went**.

Other verbs change some letters to form the past tense.
Example: The past tense of **break** is **broke**.

A **helping verb** helps to tell about the past. **Has, have** and **had** are helping verbs used with action verbs to show the action occurred in the past. The past-tense form of the irregular verb sometimes changes when a helping verb is added.

Present Tense Irregular Verb	Past Tense Irregular Verb	Past Tense Irregular Verb With Helper
go	went	have/has/had gone
see	saw	have/has/had seen
do	did	have/has/had done
bring	brought	have/has/had brought
sing	sang	have/has/had sung
drive	drove	have/has/had driven
swim	swam	have/has/had swum
sleep	slept	have/has/had slept

Directions: Choose four words from the chart. Write one sentence using the past-tense form of the verb without a helping verb. Write another sentence using the past-tense form with a helping verb.

1. _____

   _____

2. _____

   _____

3. _____

   _____

4. _____

   _____

The Irregular Verb "Be"

Be is an irregular verb. The present-tense forms of be are **be**, **am**, **is** and **are**. The past-tense forms of **be** are **was** and **were**.

Directions: Write the correct form of **be** in the blanks. The first one has been done for you.

1. I _____**am**_____ so happy for you!

2. Jared _____ unfriendly yesterday.

3. English can _____ a lot of fun to learn.

4. They _____ among the nicest people I know.

5. They _____ late yesterday.

6. She promises she _____ going to arrive on time.

7. I _____ nervous right now about the test.

8. If you _____ satisfied now, so am I.

9. He _____ as nice to me last week as I had hoped.

10. He can _____ very gracious.

11. Would you _____ offended if I moved your desk?

12. He _____ watching at the window for me yesterday.

Name: _____

Verbs: "Was" and "Were"

Singular	Plural
I was	we were
you were	you were
he, she, it was	they were

Directions: Write the correct form of the verb In the blanks. Circle the subject of each sentence. The first one has been done for you.

I was over there when it happened

You were?

____was____   1. (He) was/were so happy that we all smiled, too.

_____   2. Was/Were you at the party?

_____   3. She was/were going to the store.

_____   4. He was/were always forgetting his hat.

_____   5. Was/Were she there?

_____   6. Was/Were you sure of your answers?

_____   7. She was/were glad to help.

_____   8. They was/were excited.

_____   9. Exactly what was/were you planning to do?

_____   10. It was/were wet outside.

_____   11. They was/were scared by the noise.

_____   12. Was/Were they expected before noon?

_____   13. It was/were too early to get up!

_____   14. She was/were always early.

_____   15. You were/was the first person I asked

Name: _____

Verbs: "Went" and "Gone"

The word **went** is used without a helping verb.

Examples:

Correct: Susan **went** to the store.

Incorrect: Susan **has went** to the store.

Gone is used with a helping verb.

Examples:

Correct: Susan **has gone** to the store.

Incorrect: Susan **gone** to the store.

Directions: Write **C** in the blank if the verb is used correctly. Draw an **X** in the blank if the verb is not used correctly.

_____C_____ 1. She has gone to my school since last year.

_____ 2. Has not he been gone a long time?

_____ 3. He has went to the same class all year.

_____ 4. I have went to that doctor since I was born.

_____ 5. She is long gone!

_____ 6. Who among us has not gone to get a drink yet?

_____ 7. The class has gone on three field trips this year.

_____ 8. The class went on three field trips this year.

_____ 9. Who has not went to the board with the right answer?

_____ 10. We have not went on our vacation yet.

_____ 11. Who is went for the pizza?

_____ 12. The train has been gone for 2 hours.

_____ 13. The family had gone to the movies.

_____ 14. Have you went to visit the new bookstore?

_____ 15. He has gone on and on about how smart you are!

Name: _____

Review of Terms

Use the Glossary (pp. 106–107) or a dictionary to review the words in the word box. Use the words to complete the puzzle.

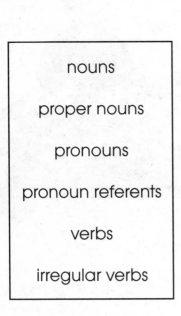

nouns

proper nouns

pronouns

pronoun referents

verbs

irregular verbs

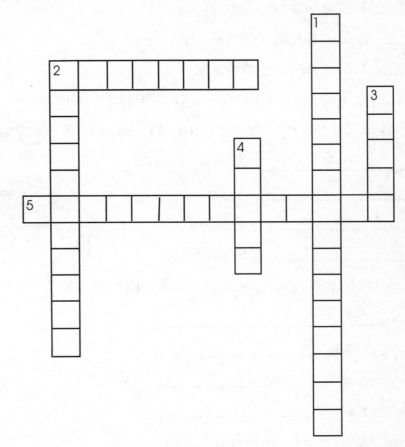

Across:

2. ____ take the place of nouns in a sentence.

5. ____ either change completely in the past tense or change some letters to form the past tense.

Down:

1. _____ the noun or nouns in a sentence that a pronoun refers to.

2. _____ name special persons, places or things. They need to be capitalized.

3. _____ name persons, places or things.

4. _____ can be either present, past or future tense.

Name: _____

Review

Directions: Write **PRES** for present tense, **PAST** for past tense or **FUT** for future tense.

_____ 1. She will help him study.

_____ 2. She helped him study.

_____ 3. She helps him study.

_____ 4. She promised she would help him study.

Directions: Write the past-tense form of these verbs.

_____ 5. cry

_____ 6. sigh

_____ 7. hurry

_____ 8. pop

Direction: Write the past tense of these irregular verbs with helpers.

9. (go) have _____

10. (sleep) have _____

11. (sing) have _____

12. (see) have _____

Directions: Write the correct form of **be**.

13. They _____ my closest neighbors.

14. I _____ very happy for you today.

15. He _____ there on time yesterday.

16. She _____ still the nicest girl I know.

Directions: Circle the correct verb.

17. He went/gone to my locker.

18. I went/gone to the beach many times.

19. Have you went/gone to this show before?

20. We went/gone all the way to the top!

Direct Objects

A **direct object** is the word or words that come after a transitive verb to complete its meaning. The direct object answers the question **whom** or **what**.

Examples:

Aaron wrote a **letter**.
Letter is the direct object. It tells what Aaron wrote.
We heard **Tom**.
Tom is the direct object. It tells whom we heard.

Directions: Identify the direct object in each sentence. Write it in the blank.

_____ 1. My mother called me.

_____ 2. The baby dropped it.

_____ 3. I met the mayor.

_____ 4. I like you!

_____ 5. No one visited them.

_____ 6. We all heard the cat.

_____ 7. Jessica saw the stars.

_____ 8. She needs a nap.

_____ 9. The dog chewed the bone.

_____ 10. He hugged the doll.

_____ 11. I sold the radio.

_____ 12. Douglas ate the banana.

_____ 13. We finally found the house.

Direct Objects

Directions: Complete each sentence by writing a direct object.

1. Eric sang _____ .

2. Our class rode _____ .

3. Jordan made _____ .

4. Keesha baked _____ .

5. All the children got _____ .

6. Our new principal read _____ .

7. My brother wrote _____ .

8. Sheree gave _____ .

9. The girls played _____ .

10. I bought _____ .

11. Mrs. Bernhard typed _____ .

12. Barb and Valerie traded _____ .

13. We all raked _____ .

14. Jennifer climbed _____ .

Name: _____

Indirect Objects

An **indirect object** is the word or words that come between the verb and the direct object. Indirect objects tells **to whom** or **what** or **for whom** or **what** something is done.

Examples:

> He read **me** a funny story.
>
> **Me** is the indirect object. It tells to whom something (reading a story) was done.
>
> She told her **mother** the truth.
>
> **Mother** is the indirect object. It tells to whom something (telling the truth) was done.

Directions: Identify the indirect object in each sentence. Write it in the blank.

1. The coach gave Bill a trophy.   _____

2. He cooked me a wonderful meal.   _____

3. She told Maria her secret.   _____

4. Someone gave my mother a gift.   _____

5. The class gave the principal a new flag for the cafeteria.   _____

6. The restaurant pays the waiter a good salary.   _____

7. You should tell your dad the truth.   _____

8. She sent her son a plane ticket.   _____

9. The waiter served the patron a salad.   _____

10. Grandma gave the baby a kiss.   _____

11. I sold Steve some cookies.   _____

12. He told us six jokes.   _____

13. She brought the boy a sucker.   _____

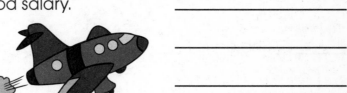

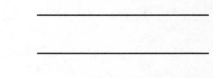

Indirect Objects

Directions: Use the words below to complete each sentence with an indirect object. The first one has been done for you.

a. the librarian	b. the coach	c. all the teachers	d. the class
e. Mom	f. the waiter	g. all of us	h. our parents

__C__ 1. The principal gave (___) the notice about the meeting.

_____ 2. My sister told (___) the truth.

_____ 3. Our teacher told (___) the homework assignment.

_____ 4. Dad bought (___) a delicious treat.

_____ 5. She gave (___) her overdue books.

_____ 6. We helped (___) clean the house.

_____ 7. The customer gave (___) a good tip.

_____ 8. Michael told (___) about his sore leg.

Name: _____

Direct and Indirect Objects

Example: Sharon told <u>Jennifer</u> a funny (story.)

Jennifer is the indirect object. It tells **to whom** Sharon told the story. Story is the direct object. It tells **what** Sharon told.

Directions: Circle the direct object in each sentence. Underline the indirect object.

1. The teacher gave the class a test.

2. Josh brought Elizabeth the book.

3. Someone left the cat a present.

4. The poet read David all his poems.

5. My big brother handed me the ticket.

6. Luke told everyone the secret.

7. Jason handed his dad the newspaper.

8. Mother bought Jack a suitcase.

9. They cooked us an excellent dinner.

10. I loaned Jonathan my bike.

11. She threw him a curve ball.

12. You tell Dad the truth!

Direct and Indirect Objects

Directions: Add a direct object and an indirect object to each sentence. Circle the direct objects and underline the indirect objects.

1. The happy clown gave _____ .

2. The smiling politician offered _____ .

3. My big brother handed _____ .

4. His uncle Seth works _____ .

5. The friendly waiter gave _____ .

6. Elizabeth told _____ .

7. My mother brought _____ .

8. He served _____ .

9. Jane should tell _____ .

10. Someone threw _____ .

11. The bookstore sent _____ .

12. The salesclerk gave _____ .

13. The magician brought _____ .

14. Her father cooked _____ .

15. His boss pays _____ .

Name: _____

More Direct and Indirect Objects

Directions: Write the direct and indirect objects in the blanks below.

1. All the girls wrote letters to their friends.

2. Each child brought the teacher an apple.

3. My Dad gave my Mom flowers on their anniversary.

4. Christopher gave the class a book report .

5. The bus drivers gave the children oranges.

6. We showed Mom the prizes.

7. My brother gave Mom and Dad his report card.

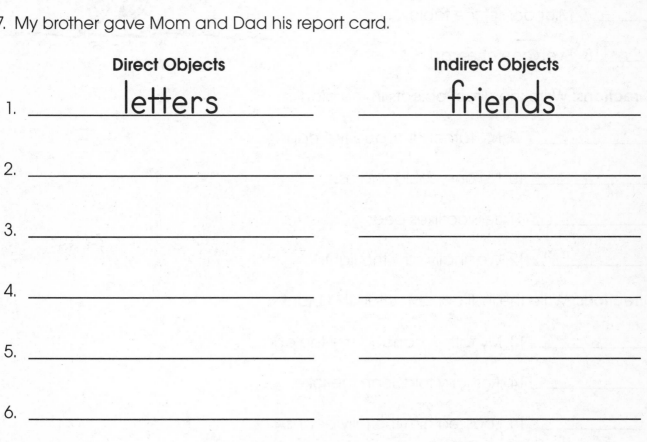

Direct Objects	Indirect Objects
1. letters	friends
2. _____	_____
3. _____	_____
4. _____	_____
5. _____	_____
6. _____	_____
7. _____	_____

Review

Directions: Identify transitive and intransitive verbs by writing a **T** or an **I** in each blank.

_____ 1. The football game was exciting.

_____ 2. No one believed her story.

_____ 3. My friend's cat meowed when I picked it up.

_____ 4. A heavy rain fell.

_____ 5. The baby cried and cried!

_____ 6. Jason polished his shoes.

_____ 7. Michael set the table.

_____ 8. Everyone cheered.

Directions: Write the direct objects in the blanks.

_____ 9. My father dropped the eggs.

_____ 10. No one could find us.

_____ 11. Jessica likes peas.

_____ 12. We finally saw the light.

Directions: Write the indirect objects in the blanks.

_____ 13. My father handed me the eggs.

_____ 14. Anthony told John the joke.

_____ 15. I passed him the jelly beans.

_____ 16. They gave us the raincoats.

Name: _____

Adverbs

Adverbs are words that tell when, where or how.

Adverbs of time tell when.

Example:

> The train left yesterday.

> **Yesterday** is an adverb of time. It tells when the train left.

Adverbs of place tell where.

Example:

> The girl walked away.

> **Away** is an adverb of place. It tells where the girl walked.

Adverbs of manner tell how.

Example:

> The boy walked quickly.

> **Quickly** is an adverb of manner. It tells how the boy walked.

Directions: Write the adverb for each sentence in the first blank. In the second blank, write whether it is an adverb of time, place or manner. The first one has been done for you.

1. The family ate downstairs.   <u>downstairs</u>   <u>place</u>

2. The relatives laughed loudly. _____ _____

3. We will finish tomorrow. _____ _____

4. The snowstorm will stop soon. _____ _____

5. She sings beautifully! _____ _____

6. The baby slept soundly. _____ _____

7. The elevator stopped suddenly. _____ _____

8. Does the plane leave today? _____ _____

9. The phone call came yesterday. _____ _____

10. She ran outside. _____ _____

Name: _____

Adverbs of Time

Directions: Choose a word or group of words from the box to complete each sentence. Make sure the adverb you choose makes sense with the rest of the sentence.

in 2 weeks	last winter
next week	at the end of the day
soon	right now
2 days ago	tonight

1. We had a surprise birthday party for him _____ .

2. Our science projects are due _____ .

3. My best friend will be moving _____ .

4. Justin and Ronnie need our help _____ !

5. We will find out who the winners are _____ .

6. Can you take me to ball practice _____ ?

7. She said we will be getting a letter _____ .

8. Diane made the quilt _____ .

Name: _____

Adverbs of Place

Directions: Choose one word from the box to complete each sentence. Make sure the adverb you choose makes sense with the rest of the sentence.

inside	upstairs	below	everywhere
home	somewhere	outside	there

1. Each child took a new library book _____ .

2. We looked _____ for his jacket.

3. We will have recess _____ because it is raining.

4. From the top of the mountain we could see the village far _____ .

5. My sister and I share a bedroom _____ .

6. The teacher warned the children, "You must play with the ball _____ ."

7. Mother said, "I know that recipe is _____ in this file box!"

8. You can put the chair _____ .

Name: _____

Adverbs of Manner

Directions: Choose a word from the box to complete each sentence. Make sure the adverb you choose makes sense with the rest of the sentence. One word will be used twice.

quickly	carefully	loudly	easily	carelessly	slowly

1. The scouts crossed the old bridge _____ .

2. We watched the turtle move _____ across the yard.

3. Everyone completed the math test _____ .

4. The quarterback scampered _____ down the sideline.

5. The mother _____ cleaned the child's sore knee.

6. The fire was caused by someone _____ tossing a match.

7. The alarm rang _____ while we were eating.

Adjectives That Add "er"

The suffix **er** is often added to adjectives to compare two things.

Example:

> My feet are **large**.
>
> Your feet are **larger** than my feet.

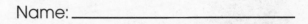

When a one-syllable adjective ends in a single consonant and the vowel is short, double the final consonant before adding **er**. When a word ends in two or more consonants, add **er**.

Examples:

> big — bigger (single consonant)
>
> bold — bolder (two consonants)

When an adjective ends in **y**, change the **y** to **i** before adding **er**.

Examples:

> easy — easier
>
> greasy — greasier
>
> breezy — breezier

Directions: Use the correct rule to add **er** to the words below. The first one has been done for you.

1. fast _____faster_____
2. thin _____
3. long _____
4. few _____
5. ugly _____
6. silly _____
7. busy _____
8. grand _____
9. lean _____
10. young _____

11. skinny _____
12. fat _____
13. poor _____
14. juicy _____
15. early _____
16. clean _____
17. thick _____
18. creamy _____
19. deep _____
20. lazy _____

Name: _____

Adjectives That Add "est"

The suffix **est** is often added to adjectives to compare more than two things.

Example:

My glass is **full**.

Your glass is **fuller**.

His glass is **fullest**.

When a one-syllable adjective ends in a single consonant and the vowel sound is short, you usually double the final consonant before adding est.

Examples:

big — biggest (short vowel)

steep — steepest (long vowel)

When an adjective ends in **y**, change the **y** to **i** before adding est.

Example:

easy — easiest

Directions: Use the correct rule to add **est** to the words below. The first one has been done for you.

1. thin   **thinnest** _____   11. quick _____

2. skinny _____   12. trim _____

3. cheap _____   13. silly _____

4. busy _____   14. tall _____

5. loud _____   15. glum _____

6. kind _____   16. red _____

7. dreamy _____   17. happy _____

8. ugly _____   18. high _____

9. pretty _____   19. wet _____

10. early _____   20. clean _____

Name: _____

Adding "er" and "est" to Adjectives

Directions: Circle the correct adjective for each sentence. The first one has been done for you.

1. Of all the students in the gym, her voice was (louder, (loudest)).

2. "I can tell you are (busier, busiest) than I am," he said to the librarian.

3. If you and Carl stand back to back, I can see which one is (taller, tallest).

4. She is the (kinder, kindest) teacher in the whole building.

5. Wow! That is the (bigger, biggest) pumpkin I have ever seen!

6. I believe your flashlight is (brighter, brightest) than mine.

7. "This is the (cleaner, cleanest) your room has been in a long time," Mother said.

8. The leaves on that plant are (prettier, prettiest) than the ones on the window sill.

Adjectives Preceded by "More"

Most adjectives of two or more syllables are preceded by the word **more** as a way to show comparison between two things.

Examples:

    Correct: intelligent, more intelligent

    Incorrect: intelligenter

    Correct: famous, more famous

    Incorrect: famouser

Directions: Write **more** before the adjectives that fit the rule. Draw an **X** in the blanks of the adjectives that do not fit the rule. To test yourself, say the words aloud using **more** and adding **er** to hear which way sounds correct. The first two have been done for you.

X	1. cheap	_____	11. awful
more	2. beautiful	_____	12. delicious
_____	3. quick	_____	13. embarrassing
_____	4. terrible	_____	14. nice
_____	5. difficult	_____	15. often
_____	6. interesting	_____	16. hard
_____	7. polite	_____	17. valuable
_____	8. cute	_____	18. close
_____	9. dark	_____	19. fast
_____	10. sad	_____	20. important

Name: _____

Adjectives Using "er" or "More"

Directions: Add the word or words needed in each sentence. The first one has been done for you.

1. I thought the book was _____ than the movie. (interesting)

2. Do you want to carry this box? It is _____ than the one you have now. (light)

3. I noticed you are moving _____ this morning. Does your ankle still bother you? (slow)

4. Thomas Edison is probably _____ for his invention of the electric light bulb than of the phonograph. (famous)

5. She stuck out her lower lip and whined, "Your ice-cream cone is _____ than mine!" (big)

6. Mom said my room was _____ than it has been in a long time. (clean)

Name: _____

Adjectives Preceded by "Most"

Most adjectives of two or more syllables are preceded by the word **most** as a way to show comparison between more than two things.

Examples:

Correct: intelligent, most intelligent
Incorrect: intelligentest
Correct: famous, most famous
Incorrect: famousest

Directions: Read the following groups of sentences. In the last sentence for each group, write the adjective preceded by **most**. The first one has been done for you.

1. My uncle is intelligent.
   My aunt is more intelligent.
   My cousin is the _____ most intelligent _____.

2. I am thankful.
   My brother is more thankful.
   My parents are the _____.

3. Your sister is polite.
   Your brother is more polite.
   You are the _____.

4. The blouse was expensive.
   The sweater was more expensive.
   The coat was the _____.

5. The class was fortunate.
   The teacher was more fortunate.
   The principal was the _____.

6. The cookies were delicious.
   The cake was even more delicious.
   The brownies were the _____.

7. That painting is elaborate.
   The sculpture is more elaborate.
   The finger painting is the _____.

Name: _____

Adjectives Using "est" or "Most"

Directions: Add the word or words needed to complete each sentence. The first one has been done for you.

1. The star over there is the _____brightest_____ of all! (bright)

2. "I believe this is the _____ time I have ever had," said Mackenzie. (delightful)

3. That game was the _____ one of the whole year! (exciting)

4. I think this tree has the _____ leaves. (green)

5. We will need the _____ knife you have to cut the face for the jack-o-lantern. (sharp)

6. Everyone agreed that your chocolate chip cookies were the _____ of all. (delicious)

Name: _____

Adjectives and Adverbs

Directions: Write **ADJ** on the line if the bold word is an adjective. Write **ADV** if the bold word is an adverb. The first one has been done for you.

_____ADV_____ 1. That road leads **nowhere**.

_____ 2. The squirrel was **nearby**.

_____ 3. Her **delicious** cookies were all eaten.

_____ 4. Everyone rushed **indoors**.

_____ 5. He **quickly** zipped his jacket.

_____ 6. She hummed a **popular** tune.

_____ 7. Her **sunny** smile warmed my heart.

_____ 8. I hung your coat **there**.

_____ 9. Bring that **here** this minute!

_____ 10. We all walked **back** to school.

_____ 11. The **skinniest** boy ate the most food!

_____ 12. She acts like a **famous** person.

_____ 13. The **silliest** jokes always make me laugh.

_____ 14. She must have parked her car **somewhere**!

_____ 15. Did you take the test **today**?

Name: _____

Adjectives and Adverbs

Directions: Read this story. Underline the adjectives. Circle the adverbs. Write the words in the correct column at the end of the story.

Surprise!

Emily and Elizabeth tiptoed quietly through the dark hallway. Even though none of the lights were lit, they knew the presents were there. Every year the two sisters had gone to Mom and Dad's bedroom to wake them on Christmas morning. This year would be different, they decided.

Last night after supper, they had secretly plotted to look early in the morning before Mom and Dad were awake. The girls knew that Emily's red-and-green stocking and Elizabeth's striped stocking hung by the brick fireplace. They knew the beautiful tree was in the corner by the rocking chair.

"Won't Mom and Dad be surprised to awaken on their own?" asked Elizabeth quietly.

Emily whispered, "Click the overhead lights so we can see better."

"You don't have to whisper," said a voice.

There sat Mom and Dad as the Christmas-tree lights suddenly shone.

Dad said, "I guess the surprise is on you two!"

Adverbs   Adjectives

_____   _____

_____   _____

_____   _____

_____   _____

_____   _____

_____   _____

_____   _____

Name: _____

Review

Directions: Write the correct words to complete the sentences. Use the words on the presents at the bottom of the page.

1. The suffix _____ and the word _____ are used when comparing two things.

2. One example of an adverb of time is _____ .

3. When an adjective ends in a consonant _____ , you change the y to i before adding er or est.

4. An _____ is a word that tells when, where or how.

5. An example of an adverb of place is _____ .

6. The suffix _____ and the word _____ are used when comparing more than two things.

7. An _____ is a word that describes a noun.

8. An example of an adverb of manner is _____ .

adjective   est   softly   adverb

er   y

most   there   more   tomorrow

Review

Directions: For the bold word in each sentence, write **N** for noun, **V** for verb, **ADJ** for adjective or **ADV** for adverb.

_____ 1. She is the **tallest** one outside.

_____ 2. **She** is the tallest one outside.

_____ 3. She **is** the tallest one outside.

_____ 4. She is the tallest one **outside**.

Directions: For the bold word in each sentence, write **P** for adverb of place, **T** for adverb of time or **M** for adverb of manner.

_____ 5. Your shoes are **downstairs**.

_____ 6. His response was **speedy**.

_____ 7. **Here** is my homework.

_____ 8. The present will be mailed **tomorrow**.

Directions: Add **er** and **est** or **more** and **most** to the words below to show comparison.

9. fat _____   _____

10. grateful _____   _____

11. serious _____   _____

12. easy _____   _____

Directions: For the bold word in each sentence, write **ADV** for adverb or **ADJ** for adjective.

_____ 13. **Grumpy** people are not pleasant.

_____ 14. Put the package **there**, please.

_____ 15. **Upstairs** is where I sleep.

_____ 16. **Warm** blankets feel toasty on cold nights.

Name: _____

"Good" and "Well"

Use the word **good** to describe a noun. Good is an adjective.

Example: She is a **good** teacher.

Use the word **well** to tell or ask how something is done or to describe someone's health. Well is an adverb. It describes a verb.

Example: She is not feeling **well**.

Directions: Write **good** or **well** in the blanks to complete the sentences correctly. The first one has been done for you.

good 1. Our team could use a good/well captain.

_____ 2. The puny kitten doesn't look good/well.

_____ 3. He did his job so good/well that everyone praised him.

_____ 4. Whining isn't a good/well habit.

_____ 5. I might just as good/well do it myself.

_____ 6. She was one of the most well-/good- liked girls at school.

_____ 7. I did the book report as good/well as I could.

_____ 8. The television works very good/well.

_____ 9. You did a good/well job repairing the TV!

_____ 10. Thanks for a job good/well done!

_____ 11. You did a good/well job fixing the computer.

_____ 12. You had better treat your friends good/well.

_____ 13. Can your grandmother hear good/well?

_____ 14. Your brother will be well/good soon.

"Your" and "You're"

The word **your** shows possession.

Examples:

Is that **your** book?

I visited **your** class.

The word **you're** is a contraction for **you are**. A **contraction** is two words joined together as one. An apostrophe shows where letters have been left out.

Examples:

You're doing well on that painting.

If you're going to pass the test, you should study.

Directions: Write **your** or **you're** on the blanks to complete the sentences correctly. The first one has been done for you.

__You're__ 1. Your/You're the best friend I have!

_____ 2. Your/You're going to drop that!

_____ 3. Your/You're brother came to see me.

_____ 4. Is that your/you're cat?

_____ 5. If your/you're going, you'd better hurry!

_____ 6. Why are your/you're fingers so red?

_____ 7. It's none of your/you're business!

_____ 8. Your/You're bike's front tire is low.

_____ 9. Your/You're kidding!

_____ 10. Have it your/you're way.

_____ 11. I thought your/you're report was great!

_____ 12. He thinks your/you're wonderful!

_____ 13. What is your/you're first choice?

_____ 14. What's your/you're opinion?

_____ 15. If your/you're going, so am I!

_____ 16. Your/You're welcome.

"Good" and "Well"; "Your" and "You're"

Directions: Choose the correct word for each sentence: **good**, **well**, **your** or **you're**.

1. "I was quite pleased with the _____ job you did on the report," said Mr. Free.

2. Our teacher said to make sure you take _____ jacket along on the trip.

3. My mother makes really _____ potato soup. You will enjoy lunch today!

4. Are you sure _____ going to be ready for the math test tomorrow?

5. We have a substitute teacher because Ms. Stigall doesn't feel _____ this afternoon.

6. Coach Jennings said that you must have _____ health card signed before you can play basketball.

Name: _____

"Good" and "Well"; "Your" and "You're"

Directions: Choose the correct word for each sentence: **good**, **well**, **your** or **you're**.

1. Are you sure you can see _____ enough to read with the lighting you have?

2. _____ going to need a paint smock when you go to art class tomorrow afternoon.

3. I can see _____ having some trouble. Can I help with that?

4. The music department needs to buy a speaker system that has _____ quality sound.

5. The principal asked, "Where is _____ hall pass?"

6. You must do the job _____ if you expect to keep it.

7. The traffic policeman said, "May I please see _____ driver's license?"

8. The story you wrote for English class was done quite _____ .

9. That radio station you listen to is a _____ one.

10. Let us know if _____ unable to attend the meeting on Saturday.

"Its" and "It's"

The word **its** shows ownership.

Examples:

> **Its** leaves have all turned green.
>
> **Its** paw was injured.

The word **it's** is a contraction for **it is**.

Examples:

> **It's** better to be early than late.
>
> **It's** not fair!

Directions: Write **its** or **it's** to complete the sentences correctly. The first one has been done for you.

_____It's_____ 1. Its/It's never too late for ice cream!

_____ 2. Its/It's eyes are already open.

_____ 3. Its/It's your turn to wash the dishes!

_____ 4. Its/It's cage was left open.

_____ 5. Its/It's engine was beyond repair.

_____ 6. Its/It's teeth were long and pointed.

_____ 7. Did you see its/it's hind legs?

_____ 8. Why do you think its/it's mine?

_____ 9. Do you think its/it's the right color?

_____ 10. Don't pet its/it's fur too hard!

_____ 11. Its/It's from my Uncle Harry.

_____ 12. Can you tell its/it's a surprise?

_____ 13. Is its/it's stall always this clean?

_____ 14. Its/It's not time to eat yet.

_____ 15. She says its/it's working now.

"Can" and "May"

The word **can** means am able to or to be able to.

Examples:

> I **can** do that for you.
> **Can** you do that for me?

The word **may** means be allowed to or permitted to. May is used to ask or give permission. **May** can also mean **might** or **perhaps**.

Examples:

> **May** I be excused?
> You **may** sit here.

Directions: Write **can** or **may** on the blanks to complete the sentences correctly. The first one has been done for you.

__May_____ 1. Can/May I help you?

_____ 2. He's smart. He can/may do it himself.

_____ 3. When can/may I have my dessert?

_____ 4. I can/may tell you exactly what she said.

_____ 5. He can/may speak French fluently.

_____ 6. You can/may use my pencil.

_____ 7. I can/may be allowed to attend the concert.

_____ 8. It's bright. I can/may see you!

_____ 9. Can/May my friend stay for dinner?

_____ 10. You can/may leave when your report is finished.

_____ 11. I can/may see your point!

_____ 12. She can/may dance well.

_____ 13. Can/May you hear the dog barking?

_____ 14. Can/May you help me button this sweater?

_____ 15. Mother, can/may I go to the movies?

Name: _____

"Its" and "It's"; "Can" and "May"

Directions: Choose the correct word for each sentence: **its**, **it's**, **can** or **may**.

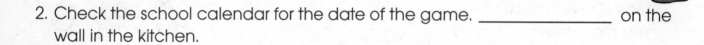

1. You need to try your best. I know you _____ do it!

2. Check the school calendar for the date of the game. _____ on the wall in the kitchen.

3. Mother said we _____ go if we get our rooms cleaned in time.

4. I realize _____ going to be a long trip. That's why I brought along a book to read on the train.

5. The puppy was chasing _____ tail.

6. We _____ not be able to have our class picnic outside because of the rain.

"Its" and "It's"; "Can" and "May"

Directions: Choose the correct word for each sentence: **its**, **it's**, **can** or **may**.

1. "It looks as though your arms are full, Diane. _____ I help you with some of those things?" asked Michele.

2. The squirrel _____ climb up the tree quickly with his mouth full of acorns.

3. She has had her school jacket so long that it is beginning to lose _____ color.

4. How many laps around the track _____ you do?

5. Sometimes you can tell what a story is going to be about by looking at _____ title.

6. Our house _____ need to be painted again in two or three years.

7. Mother asked, "Jon, _____ you open the door for your father?"

8. _____ going to be a while until your birthday, but do you know what you want?

9. I can feel it in the air; _____ going to snow soon.

10. If I'm careful with it, _____ I borrow your CD player?

"Sit" and "Set"

The word **sit** means to rest.

Examples:

> Please **sit** here!
>
> Will you **sit** by me?

The word **set** means to put or place something.

Examples:

> **Set** your purse there.
>
> **Set** the dishes on the table.

Directions: Write **sit** or **set** to complete the sentences correctly. The first one has been done for you.

_____sit_____	1. Would you please sit/set down here?
_____	2. You can sit/set the groceries there.
_____	3. She sit/set her suitcase in the closet.
_____	4. He sit/set his watch for half past three.
_____	5. She's a person who can't sit/set still.
_____	6. Sit/set the baby on the couch beside me.
_____	7. Where did you sit/set your new shoes?
_____	8. They decided to sit/set together during the movie.
_____	9. Let me sit/set you straight on that!
_____	10. Instead of swimming, he decided to sit/set in the water.
_____	11. He sit/set the greasy pan in the sink.
_____	12. She sit/set the file folder on her desk.
_____	13. Don't ever sit/set on the refrigerator!
_____	14. She sit/set the candles on the cake.
_____	15. Get ready! Get sit/set! Go!

Name: _____

"They're," "Their," "There"

The word **they're** is a contraction for **they are**.

Examples:

>**They're** our very best friends!

>Ask them if **they're** coming over tomorrow.

The word **their** shows ownership.

Examples:

>**Their** dog is friendly.

>It's **their** bicycle.

The word **there** shows place or direction.

Examples:

>Look over **there**.

>**There** it is.

Directions: Write **they're**, **their** or **there** to complete the sentences correctly. The first one has been done for you.

__There__ 1. They're/Their/There is the sweater I want!

_____ 2. Do you believe they're/their/there stories?

_____ 3. Be they're/their/there by one o'clock.

_____ 4. Were you they're/their/there last night?

_____ 5. I know they're/their/there going to attend.

_____ 6. Have you met they're/their/there mother?

_____ 7. I can go they're/their/there with you.

_____ 8. Do you like they're/their/there new car?

_____ 9. They're/Their/There friendly to everyone.

_____ 10. Did she say they're/their/there ready to go?

_____ 11. She said she'd walk by they're/their/there house.

_____ 12. Is anyone they're/their/there?

_____ 13. I put it right over they're/their/there!

Name: _____

"Sit" and "Set"; "They're," "There," "Their"

Directions: Choose the correct word for each sentence: **sit, set, they're, there** or **their**.

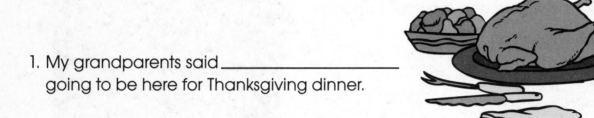

1. My grandparents said _____ going to be here for Thanksgiving dinner.

2. I heard the band director tell them to put _____ instruments away.

3. The principal said, "Please come in and _____ down."

4. He wasn't sure if he should park his bike over _____ by the fence.

5. _____ not sure how many days the trip will take.

6. Why don't you ask Aunt Peggy if she needs help to _____ the table for breakfast?

"Sit" and "Set"; "They're," "There," "Their"

Directions: Choose the correct word for each sentence: **sit**, **set**, **they're**, **there** or **their**.

1. Her muscles became tense as she heard the gym teacher say, "Get ready, get _____ , go!"

2. When we choose our seats on the bus will you _____ with me?

3. _____ is my library book! I wondered where I had left it!

4. My little brother and his friend said _____ not going to the ball game with us.

5. Before the test, the teacher wants the students to sharpen _____ pencils.

6. She blew the whistle and shouted, "Everyone _____ down on the floor!"

7. All the books for the fourth graders belong over _____ on the top shelf.

8. The little kittens are beginning to open _____ eyes.

9. I'm going to _____ the dishes on the table.

10. _____ going to be fine by themselves for a few minutes.

Name: _____

"This" and "These"

The word **this** is an adjective that refers to things that are near. **This** always describes a singular noun. Singular means one.

Example:

I'll buy **this** coat.

(Coat is singular.)

The word **these** is also an adjective that refers to things that are near. **These** always describes a plural noun. A plural refers to more than one thing.

Example:

I will buy **these** flowers.

(Flowers is a plural noun.)

Directions: Write **this** or **these** to complete the sentences correctly. The first one has been done for you.

_____these_____ 1. I will take this/these cookies with me.

_____ 2. Do you want this/these seeds?

_____ 3. Did you try this/these nuts?

_____ 4. Do it this/these way!

_____ 5. What do you know about this/these situation?

_____ 6. Did you open this/these doors?

_____ 7. Did you open this/these window?

_____ 8. What is the meaning of this/these letters?

_____ 9. Will you carry this/these books for me?

_____ 10. This/These pans are hot!

_____ 11. Do you think this/these light is too bright?

_____ 12. Are this/these boots yours?

_____ 13. Do you like this/these rainy weather?

Name: _____

Review

Directions: Complete the sentences by writing the correct words in the blanks.

_____ 1. You have a good/well attitude.

_____ 2. The teacher was not feeling good/well.

_____ 3. She sang extremely good/well.

_____ 4. Everyone said Josh was a good/well boy.

_____ 5. Your/You're going to be sorry for that!

_____ 6. Tell her your/you're serious.

_____ 7. Your/You're report was wonderful!

_____ 8. Your/You're the best person for the job.

_____ 9. Do you think its/it's going to have babies?

_____ 10. Its/It's back paw had a thorn in it.

_____ 11. Its/It's fun to make new friends.

_____ 12. Is its/it's mother always nearby?

_____ 13. How can/may I help you?

_____ 14. You can/may come in now.

_____ 15. Can/May you lift this for me?

_____ 16. She can/may sing soprano.

_____ 17. I'll wait for you to sit/set down first.

_____ 18. We sit/set our dirty boots outside.

_____ 19. It's they're/their/there turn to choose.

_____ 20. They're/Their/There is your answer!

_____ 21. They say they're/their/there coming.

_____ 22. I must have this/these one!

_____ 23. I saw this/these gloves at the store.

_____ 24. He said this/these were his.

Review

Directions: Write the correct answers in the blanks using the words in the box.

good	well	your	you're	its
it's	can	may	sit	set
they're	there	their	this	these

1. _____ is an adjective that refers to a particular thing.

2. Use _____ to tell or ask how something is done or to describe someone's health.

3. _____ is a contraction for it is.

4. _____ describes a plural noun and refers to particular things.

5. _____ means to rest.

6. _____ means am able to or to be able to.

7. _____ is a contraction for they are.

8. _____ , _____ and _____ show ownership or possession.

9. Use _____ to ask politely to be permitted to do something.

10. _____ is a contraction for you are.

11. _____ means to place or put.

12. _____ describes a noun.

13. Use _____ to show direction or placement.

Name: _____

Making Sense of Sentences

A **statement** is a sentence that tells something. It ends with a period (.).

Example: Columbus is the capital of Ohio.

A **question** is a sentence that asks something. It ends with a question mark (?).

Example: Do you like waffles?

An **exclamation** is a sentence that shows strong feeling.
It ends with an exclamation mark (!).

Example: You're the best friend in the world!

A **command** is a sentence that orders someone to do something. It ends with a period or exclamation mark.

Example: Shut the door. Watch out for that trunk!

A **request** is a sentence that asks someone to do something. It ends with a period or question mark.

Example: Please shut the door.

Directions: Write **S** if the sentence makes a statement, **Q** if it asks a question, **E** if it is an exclamation, **C** if it issues a command or **R** if it makes a request. Punctuate each sentence correctly.

_____ 1. Please open your mouth

_____ 2. Will you be going to the party

_____ 3. That's hot

_____ 4. Give me the car keys right now

_____ 5. Do you think she will run fast

_____ 6. It's cold today

_____ 7. You're incredible

_____ 8. Run for your life

_____ 9. Is today the deadline

_____ 10. I turned in my paper early

_____ 11. Call the doctor immediately

_____ 12. Turn around and touch your toes

_____ 13. Be at my house at noon tomorrow

_____ 14. Give me a clue

_____ 15. Can you give me a clue

_____ 16. Please wipe your face

_____ 17. It's time for me to go home

_____ 18. No one believed what she said

_____ 19. Are you interested

_____ 20. He's badly hurt

Name: _____

Writing Question Sentences

Directions: Rewrite each sentence to make it a question. The first one has been done for you. In some cases, the form of the verb must be changed.

1. She slept soundly all day.

<u>Did she sleep soundly all day?</u>

2. The cookies are hot.

_____

3. He put the cake in the oven.

_____

4. She lives in the green house.

_____

5. He understood my directions.

_____

6. Jessica ran faster than anyone.

_____

7. The bus was gone before he arrived.

_____

8. His car is yellow.

_____

9. Elizabeth wants some more beans.

_____

82

Name: _____

Conjunctions

Words that join sentences or combine ideas like **and, but, or, because, when, after** and **so** are called **conjunctions**.

Examples:

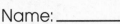

I played the drums, **and** Sue played the clarinet.
She likes bananas, **but** I do not.
We could play music **or** just enjoy the silence.
I needed the book **because** I had to write a book report.
He gave me the book **when** I asked for it.
I asked her to eat lunch **after** she finished the test.
You wanted my bike **so** you could ride it.

Using different conjunctions can affect the meaning of a sentence.

Example:

He gave me the book **when** I asked for it.
He gave me the book **after** I asked for it.

Directions: Choose the best conjunction to combine the pairs of sentences. The first one has been done for you.

1. I like my hair curly. Mom likes my hair straight.

<u>I like my hair curly, but Mom likes it straight.</u>

2. I can remember what she looks like. I can't remember her name.

_____

3. We will have to wash the dishes. We won't have clean plates for dinner.

_____

4. The yellow flowers are blooming. The red flowers are not.

_____

5. I like banana cream pie. I like chocolate donuts.

_____

Name: _____

"And," "But," "Or"

Directions: Write **and**, **but** or **or** to complete the sentences.

1. I thought we might try that new hamburger place, _____ Mom wants to eat at the Spaghetti Shop.

2. We could stay home, _____ would you rather go to the game?

3. She went right home after school, _____ he stopped at the store.

4. Mother held the piece of paneling, _____ Father nailed it in place.

5. She babysat last weekend, _____ her big sister went with her.

6. She likes raisins in her oatmeal, _____ I would rather have mine with brown sugar.

7. She was planning on coming over tomorrow, _____ I asked her if she could wait until the weekend.

8. Tomato soup with crackers sounds good to me, _____ would you rather have vegetable beef soup?

Name: _____

"Because" and "So"

Directions: Write **because** or **so** to complete the sentences.

1. She cleaned the paint brushes _____ they would be ready in the morning.

2. Father called home complaining of a sore

   throat _____ Mom stopped by the pharmacy.

3. His bus will be running late _____ it has a flat tire.

4. We all worked together _____ we could get the job done sooner.

5. We took a variety of sandwiches on the picnic _____ we knew not everyone liked cheese and olives with mayonnaise.

6. All the school children were sent home _____ the electricity went off at school.

7. My brother wants us to meet his girlfriend _____ she will be coming to dinner with us on Friday.

8. He forgot to take his umbrella along this morning _____ now his clothes are very wet.

Name: _____

"When" and "After"

Directions: Write **when** or **after** to complete the sentences.

1. I knew we were in trouble _____ I heard the thunder in the distance.

2. We carried the baskets of cherries to the car _____ we were finished picking them.

3. Mother took off her apron _____ I reminded her that our dinner guests would be here any minute.

4. I wondered if we would have school tomorrow _____ I noticed the snow begin to fall.

5. The boys and girls all clapped _____ the magician pulled the colored scarves out of his sleeve.

6. I was startled _____ the phone rang so late last night.

7. You will need to get the film developed _____ you have taken all the pictures.

8. The children began to run _____ the snake started to move!

Name: _____

Conjunctions

Directions: Choose the best conjunction from the box to combine the pairs of sentences. Then rewrite the sentences.

| and | but | or | because | when | after | so |

1. I like Leah. I like Ben.

_____

2. Should I eat the orange? Should I eat the apple?

_____

3. You will get a reward. You turned in the lost item.

_____

4. I really mean what I say! You had better listen!

_____

5. I like you. You're nice, friendly, helpful and kind.

_____

6. You can have dessert. You ate all your peas.

_____

7. I like your shirt better. You should decide for yourself.

_____

8. We walked out of the building. We heard the fire alarm.

_____

9. I like to sing folk songs. I like to play the guitar.

_____

Name: _____

Run-On Sentences

A **run-on sentence** occurs when two or more sentences are joined together without punctuation.

Examples:

Run-on sentence: I lost my way once did you?

Two sentences with correct punctuation: I lost my way once. Did you?

Run-on sentence: I found the recipe it was not hard to follow.

Two sentences with correct punctuation: I found the recipe. It was not hard to follow.

Directions: Rewrite the run-on sentences correctly with periods, exclamation points and question marks. The first one has been done for you.

1. Did you take my umbrella I can't find it anywhere!

Did you take my umbrella? I can't find it anywhere!

2. How can you stand that noise I can't!

_____

3. The cookies are gone I see only crumbs.

_____

4. The dogs were barking they were hungry.

_____

5. She is quite ill please call a doctor immediately!

_____

6. The clouds came up we knew the storm would hit soon.

_____

7. You weren't home he stopped by this morning.

_____

Name: _____

Combining Sentences

Some simple sentences can be easily combined into one sentence.

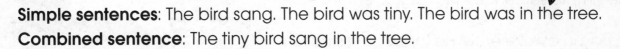

Examples:

    Simple sentences: The bird sang. The bird was tiny. The bird was in the tree.
    Combined sentence: The tiny bird sang in the tree.

Directions: Combine each set of simple sentences into one sentence. The first one has been done for you.

1. The big girls laughed. They were friendly. They helped the little girls.

The big, friendly girls laughed as they helped the little girls.

2. The dog was hungry. The dog whimpered. The dog looked at its bowl.

_____

3. Be quiet now. I want you to listen. You listen to my joke!

_____

4. I lost my pencil. My pencil was stubby. I lost it on the bus.

_____

5. I see my mother. My mother is walking. My mother is walking down the street.

_____

6. Do you like ice cream? Do you like hot dogs? Do you like mustard?

_____

7. Tell me you'll do it! Tell me you will! Tell me right now!

_____

Combining Sentences in Paragraph Form

A **paragraph** is a group of sentences that share the same idea.

Directions: Rewrite the paragraph by combining the simple sentences into larger sentences.

Jason awoke early. He threw off his covers. He ran to his window. He looked outside. He saw snow. It was white and fluffy. Jason thought of something. He thought of his sled. His sled was in the garage. He quickly ate breakfast. He dressed warmly. He got his sled. He went outside. He went to play in the snow.

_____

_____

_____

_____

_____

_____

_____

_____

_____

_____

_____

_____

_____

Name: _____

Review

Directions: Write **S** for statement, **R** for request, **C** for command, **Q** for question or **E** for exclamation.

_____ 1. Please hand me that tool.

_____ 2. Give me that hammer.

_____ 3. That hurts!

_____ 4. The class meets at noon today.

_____ 5. Will you be at the meeting?

_____ 6. Open your fingers wide.

Directions: Rewrite these sentences as questions.

7. Please come here. _____

8. He wondered where we were. _____

Directions: Rewrite these run-on sentences correctly with periods, exclamation marks or question marks.

9. I won't bother you I'll just wait. _____

10. Trust me I'm a true friend. _____

Directions: Combine and rewrite these sets of simple sentences.

11. The baby was cheerful. The baby was smiling. The baby was a joy to be around.

_____

12. I lost my hammer. I lost my nails. I lost my patience.

_____

Directions: Use conjunctions to combine these sentences.

13. I like ripe bananas. He likes green bananas.

_____

14. I will add up the charges. I will tell you the costs.

_____

Punctuation: Commas

Use a comma to separate the number of the day of a month and the year. Do not use a comma to separate the month and year if no day is given.

Examples:

June 14, 1999

June 1999

Use a comma after **yes** or **no** when it is the first word in a sentence.

Examples:

Yes, I will do it right now.

No, I don't want any.

Directions: Write **C** if the sentence is punctuated correctly. Draw an **X** if the sentence is not punctuated correctly. The first one has been done for you.

__C__ 1. No, I don't plan to attend.

_____ 2. I told them, oh yes, I would go.

_____ 3. Her birthday is March 13, 1995.

_____ 4. He was born in May, 1997.

_____ 5. Yes, of course I like you!

_____ 6. No I will not be there.

_____ 7. They left for vacation on February, 14.

_____ 8. No, today is Monday.

_____ 9. The program was first shown on August 12, 1991.

_____ 10. In September, 2007 how old will you be?

_____ 11. He turned 12 years old on November, 13.

_____ 12. I said no, I will not come no matter what!

_____ 13. Yes, she is a friend of mine.

_____ 14. His birthday is June 12, 1992, and mine is June 12, 1993.

_____ 15. No I would not like more dessert.

Name: _____

Punctuation: Commas

Use a comma to separate words in a series. A comma is used after each word in a series but is not needed before the last word. Both ways are correct. In your own writing, be consistent about which style you use.

Examples:

   We ate apples, oranges, and pears.
   We ate apples, oranges and pears.

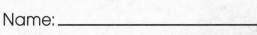

Always use a comma between the name of a city and a state.

Example:

   She lives in Fresno, California.
   He lives in Wilmington, Delaware.

Directions: Write **C** if the sentence is punctuated correctly. Draw an **X** if the sentence is not punctuated correctly. The first one has been done for you.

___X___   1. She ordered shoes, dresses and shirts to be sent to her home in Oakland California.

_____   2. No one knew her pets' names were Fido, Spot and Tiger.

_____   3. He likes green beans lima beans, and corn on the cob.

_____   4. Typing paper, pens and pencils are all needed for school.

_____   5. Send your letters to her in College Park, Maryland.

_____   6. Orlando Florida is the home of Disney World.

_____   7. Mickey, Minnie, Goofy and Daisy are all favorites of mine.

_____   8. Send your letter to her in Reno, Nevada.

_____   9. Before he lived in New York, City he lived in San Diego, California.

_____   10. She mailed postcards, and letters to him in Lexington, Kentucky.

_____   11. Teacups, saucers, napkins, and silverware were piled high.

_____   12. Can someone give me a ride to Indianapolis, Indiana?

_____   13. He took a train a car, then a boat to visit his old friend.

_____   14. Why can't I go to Disney World to see Mickey, and Minnie?

Name: _____

Punctuation: Quotation Marks

Use quotation marks (" ") before and after the exact words of a speaker.

Examples:

I asked Aunt Martha, "How do you feel?"

"I feel awful," Aunt Martha replied.

Do not put quotation marks around words that report what the speaker said.

Examples:

Aunt Martha said she felt awful.

I asked Aunt Martha how she felt.

Directions: Write **C** if the sentence is punctuated correctly. Draw an **X** if the sentence is not punctuated correctly. The first one has been done for you.

_C_ 1. "I want it right now!" she demanded angrily.

_____ 2 "Do you want it now? I asked."

_____ 3. She said "she felt better" now.

_____ 4. Her exact words were, "I feel much better now!"

_____ 5. "I am so thrilled to be here!" he shouted.

_____ 6. "Yes, I will attend," she replied.

_____ 7. Elizabeth said "she was unhappy."

_____ 8. "I'm unhappy," Elizabeth reported.

_____ 9. "Did you know her mother?" I asked.

_____ 10. I asked "whether you knew her mother."

_____ 11. I wondered, "What will dessert be?"

_____ 12. "Which will it be, salt or pepper?" the waiter asked.

_____ 13. "No, I don't know the answer!" he snapped.

_____ 14. He said "yes he'd take her on the trip.

_____ 15. Be patient, he said. "it will soon be over."

Name: _____

Punctuation: Quotation Marks

Use quotation marks around the titles of songs and poems.

Examples:

Have you heard "Still Cruising" by the Beach Boys?

"Ode To a Nightingale" is a famous poem.

Directions: Write **C** if the sentence is punctuated correctly. Draw an **X** if the sentence is not punctuated correctly. The first one has been done for you.

__C__ 1. Do you know "My Bonnie Lies Over the Ocean"?

_____ 2. We sang The Stars and Stripes Forever" at school.

_____ 3. Her favorite song is "The Eensy Weensy Spider."

_____ 4. Turn the music up when "A Hard Day's "Night comes on!

_____ 5. "Yesterday" was one of Paul McCartney's most famous songs.

_____ 6. "Mary Had a Little Lamb" is a very silly poem!

_____ 7. A song everyone knows is "Happy Birthday."

_____ 8. "Swing Low, Sweet Chariot" was first sung by slaves.

_____ 9. Do you know the words to Home on "the Range"?

_____10. "Hiawatha" is a poem many older people had to memorize.

_____11. "Happy Days Are Here Again! is an upbeat tune.

_____12. Frankie Valli and the Four Seasons sang "Sherry."

_____13. The words to "Rain, Rain" Go Away are easy to learn.

_____14. A slow song I know is called "Summertime."

_____15. Little children like to hear "The Night Before Christmas."

Name: _____

Book Titles

All words in the title of a book are underlined. Underlined words also mean italics.

Examples:

The Hunt for Red October was a best-seller!
(*The Hunt for Red October*)

Have you read Lost in Space? (*Lost in Space*)

Directions: Underline the book titles in these sentences.
The first one has been done for you.

1. The Dinosaur Poster Book is for eight year olds.

2. Have you read Lion Dancer by Kate Waters?

3. Baby Dinosaurs and Giant Dinosaurs were both written by Peter Dodson.

4. Have you heard of the book That's What Friends Are For by Carol Adorjan?

5. J.B. Stamper wrote a book called The Totally Terrific Valentine Party Book.

6. The teacher read Almost Ten and a Half aloud to our class.

7. Marrying Off Mom is about a girl who tries to get her widowed mother to start dating.

8. The Snow and The Fire are the second and third books by author Caroline Cooney.

9. The title sounds silly, but Goofbang Value Daze really is the name of a book!

10. A book about space exploration is The Day We Walked on the Moon by George Sullivan.

11. Alice and the Birthday Giant tells about a giant who came to a girl's birthday party.

12. A book about a girl who is sad about her father's death is called Rachel and the Upside Down Heart by Eileen Douglas.

13. Two books about baseball are Baseball Bloopers and Oddball Baseball.

14. Katharine Ross wrote Teenage Mutant Ninja Turtles: The Movie Storybook.

Book Titles

Capitalize the first and last word of book titles. Capitalize all other words of book titles except short prepositions, such as **of**, **at** and **in**; conjunctions, such as **and**, **or** and **but**; and articles, such as **a**, **an** and **the**.

Examples:

Have you read <u>War and Peace</u>?

Pippi Longstocking in Moscow is her favorite book.

Directions: Underline the book titles. Circle the words that should be capitalized. The first one has been done for you.

1. ⟨murder⟩ in the ⟨blue room⟩ by Elliot Roosevelt

2. growing up in a divided society by Sandra Burnham

3. the corn king and the spring queen by Naomi Mitchison

4. new kids on the block by Grace Catalano

5. best friends don't tell lies by Linda Barr

6. turn your kid into a computer genius by Carole Gerber

7. 50 simple things you can do to save the earth by Earth Works Press

8. garfield goes to waist by Jim Davis

9. the hunt for red october by Tom Clancy

10. fall into darkness by Christopher Pike

11. oh the places you'll go! by Dr. Seuss

12. amy the dancing bear by Carly Simon

13. the great waldo search by Martin Handford

14. the time and space of uncle albert by Russel Stannard

15. true stories about abraham lincoln by Ruth Gross

Capital Letters and Periods

The first letter of a person's first, last and middle name is always capitalized.

Example: Elizabeth **J**ane **M**arks is my best friend.

The first letter of a person's title is always capitalized.
If the title is abbreviated, the title is followed by a period.

Examples: Her mother is **Dr**. Susan Jones Marks.
Ms. Jessica Joseph was a visitor.

C if the sentence is punctuated and capitalized correctly.
Draw an **X** if the sentence is not punctuated and capitalized correctly. The first one has been done for you.

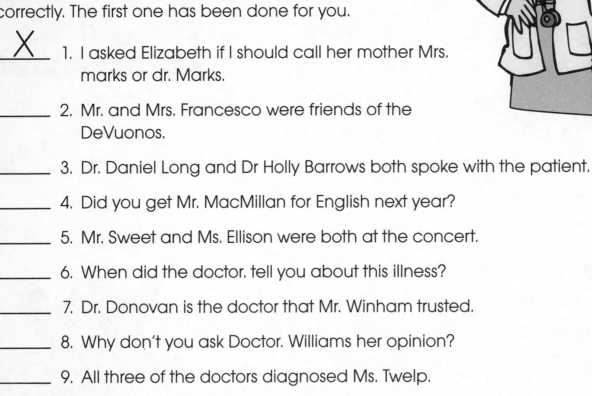

_X___ 1. I asked Elizabeth if I should call her mother Mrs. marks or dr. Marks.

_____ 2. Mr. and Mrs. Francesco were friends of the DeVuonos.

_____ 3. Dr. Daniel Long and Dr Holly Barrows both spoke with the patient.

_____ 4. Did you get Mr. MacMillan for English next year?

_____ 5. Mr. Sweet and Ms. Ellison were both at the concert.

_____ 6. When did the doctor. tell you about this illness?

_____ 7. Dr. Donovan is the doctor that Mr. Winham trusted.

_____ 8. Why don't you ask Doctor. Williams her opinion?

_____ 9. All three of the doctors diagnosed Ms. Twelp.

_____10. Will Ms. Davis and Ms Simpson be at school today?

_____11. Did Dr Samuels see your father last week?

_____12. Is Judy a medical doctor or another kind of specialist?

_____13. We are pleased to introduce Ms King and Mr. Graham.

Name: _____

Review

Directions: The following sentences have errors in punctuation, capitalization or both. The number in parentheses **( )** at the end of each sentence tells you how many errors it contains. Correct the errors by rewriting each sentence.

1. I saw mr. Johnson reading War And Peace to his class. (2)

_____

2. Do you like to sing "Take me Out to The Ballgame"? (2)

_____

3. He recited Hiawatha to Miss. Simpson's class. (2)

_____

4. Bananas, and oranges are among Dr smith's favorite fruits. (3)

_____

5. "Daisy, daisy is a song about a bicycle built for two. (2)

_____

6. Good Morning, Granny Rose is about a woman and her dog. (1)

_____

7. Garfield goes to waist is a very funny book! (3)

_____

8. Peanut butter, jelly, and bread are Miss. Lee's favorite treats. (1)

_____

Name: _____

Proofreading

Proofreading means searching for and correcting errors by carefully reading and rereading what has been written. Use the proofreading marks below when correcting your writing or someone else's.

To insert a word or a punctuation mark that has been left out, use this mark: ∧. It is called a caret.

Example: We ∧ to the dance together.
     went

To show that a letter should be capitalized, put three lines under it.

Example: Mrs. jones drove us to school.

To show that a capital letter should be a small or lower-case, draw a diagonal line through it.

Example: Mrs. Jones Drove us to school.

To show that a word is spelled incorrectly, draw a horizontal line through it and write the correct spelling above it.

Example: The ~~wolros~~ is an amazing animal.
        walrus

Directions: Proofread the two paragraphs using the proofreading marks you learned. The author's last name, Towne, is spelled correctly.

The Modern ark

My book report is on the modern ark by Cecilia Fitzsimmons. The book tells abut 80 of worlds endangered animals. The book also an arc and animals inside for kids put together.

Their House

there house is a Great book! The arthur's name is Mary Towne. they're house tells about a girl name Molly. Molly's Family bys an old house from some people named warren. Then there big problems begin!

Name: _____

Proofreading

Directions: Proofread the paragraphs, using the proofreading marks you learned. There are seven capitalization errors, three missing words and eleven errors in spelling or word usage.

Key West

key West has been tropical paradise ever since Ponce de Leon first saw the set of islands called the keys in 1513. Two famus streets in Key West are named duval and whitehead. You will find the city semetery on Francis Street. The tombstones are funny!

The message on one is, "I told you I was sick!" On sailor's tombston is this mesage his widow: "At lease I no where to find him now."

The cemetery is on 21 akres in the midle of town. The most famous home in key west is that of the authur, Ernest Hemingway. Heminway's home was at 907 whitehead Street. He lived their for 30 years.

Name: _____

Proofreading

Directions: Read more about Key West. Proofread and correct the errors. There are eight errors in capitalization, seven misspelled words, a missing comma and three missing words.

More About Key West

a good way to lern more about key West is to ride the trolley. Key West has a great troley system. The trolley will take on a tour of the salt ponds. You can also three red brick forts. The troley tour goes by a 110-foot high lighthouse. It is rite in the middle of the city. Key west is the only city with a Lighthouse in the midle of it! It is also the southernmost city in the United States.

If you have time, the new Ship Wreck Museum. Key west was also the hom of former president Harry truman. During his presidency, Trueman spent many vacations on key west.

Name: _____

Proofreading

Directions: Proofread the sentences. Write **C** if the sentence has no errors. Draw an **X** if the sentence contains missing words or other errors. The first one has been done for you.

__C__ 1. The new Ship Wreck Museum in Key West is exciting!

_____ 2. Another thing I liked was the litehouse.

_____ 3. Do you remember Hemingway's address in Key West?

_____ 4. The Key West semetery is on 21 acres of ground.

_____ 5. Ponce de eon discovered Key West.

_____ 6. The cemetery in Key West is on Francis Street.

_____ 7. My favorete tombstone was the sailor's.

_____ 8. His wife wrote the words on it. Remember?

_____ 9. The words said, "at least I know where to find him now!"

_____ 10. That sailor must have been away at sea all the time.

_____ 11. The troley ride around Key West is very interesting.

_____ 12. Do you why it is called Key West?

_____ 13. Can you imagine a lighthouse in the middle of your town?

_____ 14. It's interesting to no that Key West is our southernmost city.

_____ 15. Besides Harry Truman and Hemingway, did other famous people live there?

Proofreading

Directions: Each of the following sentences has a word missing. Use a caret to insert the missing word. The first one has been done for you.

This summer I am going to Lake Powell.

Key

1. Have you ever ridden the trolley around West?

2. The Key West lighthouse 110 feet high.

3. Ponce de Leon first the Keys in 1513.

4. Two famous streets in Key West named Duval and Whitehead.

5. The most famous home in Key West that of Ernest Hemingway.

6. The cemetery in Key West on 21 acres.

7. It is located the middle of town.

8. What strange place for a cemetery!

9. Many of the tombstones funny!

10. The funniest one has message from a widow of a sailor.

Review

Directions: Use the correct proofreading marks to show the two capitalization errors in each sentence.

1. Mrs. edwards drove us to edison Elementary School.

2. Who can Say what john's real problem was?

3. Did You tell dr. Lynn we would be there at noon?

4. My Aunt Nellie was there and so was aunt susan.

Directions: Use the correct proofreading mark to insert the missing word or letter in each sentence.

5. He promised me he be there on time!

6. Who tell me the answer to the first problem?

7. What his nickname when he was a baby?

8. Did he tell you same thing?

Directions: Use the correct proofreading mark, then correct the misspelled or misused word in each sentence.

9. I wondered if the princepal knew what had happened.

10. I herd her whole family was there!

11. Our team easley beat the other team.

12. Don't laugh to hard at those silly jokes!

Glossary

Adjective: A word that describes a noun. Examples: **fuzzy** sweater, **green** car, **nice** boy.

Adverb: A word that tells when, where or how. Example: The train will leave **early**.

Command: A sentence that orders someone to do something. It ends with a period or exclamation mark.

Compound Predicate: A predicate with two parts joined by the word **and** or another conjunction.

Compound Subject: A subject with two parts joined by the word **and** or another conjunction.

Conjunction: A word that joins sentences or combines ideas. **And, but, or, because, when, after** and **so** are conjunctions.

Contraction: Two words joined together as one. An apostrophe shows where some letters have been left out. Example: cannot — can't.

Direct Object: The word or words that come after a transitive verb to complete its meaning. It answers the question **whom** or **what**.

Exclamation: A sentence that shows strong feeling. It ends with an exclamation mark (!).

Future-Tense Verb: A verb form that tells what is going to happen. Examples: I **will be** happy. She **will run** fast.

Indirect Object: The word or words that come between the verb and the direct object. Indirect objects tell **to whom** or **what** or **for whom** or **what** something is done.

Intransitive Verb: A verb that can stand alone in the predicate because its meaning is complete. Examples: I **help**. You **play**.

Noun: A word that names a person, place or thing. Examples: **boy, town, radish**.

Paragraph: A group of sentences that share the same idea.

Past-Tense Verb: A verb form that tells what has already happened. Example: I **was** happy.

Plural: A word that refers to more than one thing.

Predicate: The part of the sentence that tells what the subject does, did, is doing or will do. Example: I **am happy**.

Present-Tense Verb: A verb form that tells what is happening now.

Pronoun: A word that takes the place of a noun. Examples: **I, me, my, he, she, it, we, us, their, them**.

Pronoun Referent: The noun or nouns that a pronoun refers to.

Proofreading: Searching for and correcting errors by carefully reading and rereading what has been written.

Proper Noun: Name of specific persons, places or things. Examples: Abe Lincoln, Empire State Building, Magna Carta.

Question: A sentence that asks something. It ends with a question mark (?).

Request: A sentence that asks someone to do something. It ends with a period or question mark.

Run-On Sentence: A run-on sentence occurs when two or more sentences are joined together without punctuation.

Sentence: A group of words that expresses a complete thought. It must have at least one subject and one verb.

Singular: A word that refers to only one thing.

Statement: A sentence that tells something. It ends with a period (.).

Subject: The part of the sentence that tells who or what the sentence is about.

Transitive Verb: A verb that needs a direct object to complete its meaning.

Verb: A word that tells what something does or that something exists.
Example: Pete **ran** down the street.

Answer Key

Identifying the Parts of a Sentence

The **subject** tells who or what the sentence is about. The subject is always a noun or pronoun. A **noun** is a word that names a person, place or thing. A **pronoun** is a word that takes the place of a noun.

Example:
The handsome **boy** danced yesterday.
Boy is the subject. The sentence is about the boy.
A verb tells what something does or that something exists.

Example:
The handsome boy **danced** yesterday.
Danced is the verb. It shows action.
An adverb tells when, where or how something happened.

Example:
The handsome boy danced **yesterday**.
Yesterday is an adverb. It tells when the boy danced.
An adjective describes a noun.

Example:
The **handsome** boy danced yesterday.
Handsome is an adjective. It describes the noun **boy**.

Directions: Write **N** for noun, **V** for verb, **ADJ** for adjective or **ADV** for adverb for the bold word in each sentence.

ADJ 1. She is an **excellent** singer.
N 2. The huge black **horse** easily won the race.
ADJ 3. The **red-haired** girl was shy.
ADV 4. Joshua **quickly** finished his homework and went out to play.
N 5. **Carrots** are my least favorite vegetable.
N 6. Why should I always have to take out the trash?
V 7. That girl **ran** like the wind!
V 8. Elizabeth **told** her sister to pick her up at noon.
ADJ 9. He was glad he had a **warm** coat to wear.
ADV 10. I live **nearby**.

3

Nouns

A noun names a person, place or thing.

Examples:

person — sister, uncle, boy, woman
place — building, city, park, street
thing — workbook, cat, candle, bed

Directions: Circle the nouns in each sentence. The first one has been done for you.

1. The (dog) ran into the (street.)
2. Please take this (book) to the (librarian.)
3. The red (apples) are in the (kitchen.)
4. That (scarf) belongs to the bus (driver.)
5. Get some blue (paper) from the (office) to make a (card.)
6. Look at the (parachute!)
7. Autumn (leaves) are beautiful.
8. The (lion) roared loudly at the (visitors.)

Directions: Write the nouns you circled in the correct group.

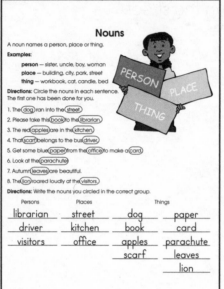

Persons	Places	Things	
librarian	street	dog	paper
driver	kitchen	book	card
visitors	office	apples	parachute
		scarf	leaves
			lion

4

Nouns

Directions: Write nouns that name persons.

1. Could you please give this report to my _____?

2. The _____ works many long hours to plant crops.

3. I had to help my little _____ when he wrecked his bike yesterday.

Directions: Write nouns that name places.

4. I always keep my library books on top of the _____ so I can find them.

5. We enjoyed watching the kites fly ~~in the~~

6. Dad built a nice _____ to keep us warm.

Directions: Write ~~nouns that~~ name things.

7. The little _____ purred softly as I held it.

8. Wouldn't you think a _____ would get tired of carrying its house around all day?

9. The _____ scurried into its hole with the piece of cheese.

10. I can tell by the writing that this _____ is mine.

11. Look at the _____ I made in art.

12. His _____ blew away because of the strong wind.

Answers will vary.

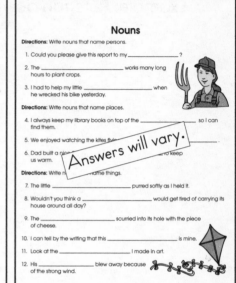

5

Proper Nouns

Proper nouns name specific persons, places or things.

Examples:

person — Ms. Steiner, Judge Jones, Lt. Raydon
place — Crestview School, California, China
thing — Declaration of Independence, Encyclopedia Britannica

Directions: Circle the proper noun in each sentence. Write person, place or thing in the blank. The first one has been done for you.

1. I returned the overdue book to the (Ashland Public Library.)

Ashland Public Library   place

2. Our new principal is (Mrs. Denes.)

Mrs. Denes   person

3. We enjoyed shopping at (Brookland Mall.)

Brookland Mall   place

4. Did you finish your report on (Charlotte's Web?)

Charlotte's Web   thing

5. The new student in our class lives on (Reed Road.)

Reed Road   place

6. (Mr. Wilkes) said he likes his new job.

Mr. Wilkes   person

7. How do you get to (Millsboro) from here?

Millsboro   place

6

Proper Nouns in Sentences

Directions: Choose the proper noun from the box to complete each sentence. Then write person, place or thing to describe the type of proper noun.

Michael Jordan	Washington Monument	Empire State Building
Titanic	Grayson Avenue School	Mark McGwire	Fruity-Juice

1. The Empire State Building used to be the tallest building in the United States.

thing

2. There was a movie made about the Titanic, one of the largest ocean liners built.

thing

3. Mark McGwire hit a record number of home runs during the regular season in 1998.

person

4. Would you trade this basketball card for your Michael Jordan card? He is my favorite basketball player!

person

5. I can't wait for lunch! Mom packed some Fruity-Juice for me to drink.

thing

6. Grayson Avenue School is my new school. All the teachers there are very friendly.

place

7

Proper Nouns: Capitalization

Proper nouns always begin with a capital letter.

Examples:

Monday
Texas
Karen
Mr. Logan
Hamburger Avenue
Rover

Directions: Cross out the lower-case letters at the beginning of the proper nouns. Write capital letters above them. The first one has been done for you

1. My teddy bear's name is ̶C̶ocoa.
2. ̶M̶s. ̶B̶ernhard does an excellent job at ̶C̶restview ̶E̶lementary ̶S̶chool.
3. ̶E̶mily, ̶E̶lizabeth and ̶M̶egan live on ̶M̶ain ̶S̶treet.
4. I am sure our teacher said the book report is due on ̶M̶onday.
5. I believe you can find ̶L̶ike ̶S̶treet if you turn left at the next light.
6. Will your family be able join our family for dinner at ̶B̶urger ̶B̶arn?
7. The weather forecasters think the storm will hit the coast of ̶L̶ouisiana ̶F̶riday afternoon.
8. My family went to ̶W̶ashington, ̶D̶̶C̶ this summer.
9. Remember, we don't have school on ̶T̶uesday because of the teachers' meeting.
10. Who do you think will win the game, the ̶C̶ougars or the ̶A̶rrows?

8

Pronouns

A **pronoun** is a word that takes the place of a noun in a sentence.

Examples:

I, my, mine, me
we, our, ours, us
you, your, yours
he, his, him
she, her, hers
it, its
they, their, theirs, them

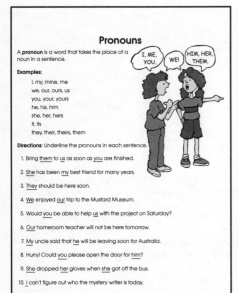

I, ME, YOU. WE! HIM, HER, THEM.

Directions: Underline the pronouns in each sentence.

1. Bring them to us as soon as you are finished.

2. She has been my best friend for many years.

3. They should be here soon.

4. We enjoyed our trip to the Mustard Museum.

5. Would you be able to help us with the project on Saturday?

6. Our homeroom teacher will not be here tomorrow.

7. My uncle said that he will be leaving soon for Australia.

8. Hurry! Could you please open the door for him?

9. She dropped her gloves when she got off the bus.

10. I can't figure out who the mystery writer is today.

9

Nouns and Pronouns

To make a story or report more interesting, pronouns can be substituted for "overused" nouns.

Example:

Mother made the beds. Then Mother started the laundry.

The noun **Mother** is used in both sentences. The pronoun **she** could be used in place of **Mother** the second time to make the second sentence more interesting.

Directions: Cross out nouns when they appear a second and/or third time. Write a pronoun that could be used instead. The first one has been done for you.

_we_ 1. My friends and I like to go ice skating in the winter. ~~My friends and I~~ usually fall down a lot, but ~~my friends and I~~ have fun!

they 2. All the children in the fourth-grade class next to us must have been having a party. ~~All the children~~ were very loud. ~~All the children~~ were happy it was Friday.

_he_ 3. I try to help my father with work around the house on the weekends. ~~My father~~ works many hours during the week and would not be able to get everything done.

they 4. Can I share my birthday treat with the secretary and the principal? The ~~secretary and the principal~~ could probably use a snack right now!

him 5. I know Mr. Jones needs a copy of this history report. Please take it to ~~Mr. Jones~~ when you finish.

10

Nouns and Pronouns

Directions: Cross out nouns when they appear a second and/or third time. Write a pronoun that could be used instead.

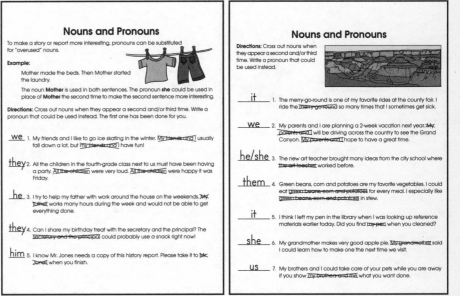

_it_ 1. The merry-go-round is one of my favorite rides at the county fair. I ride the ~~merry-go-round~~ so many times that I sometimes get sick.

_we_ 2. My parents and I are planning a 2-week vacation next year. ~~My parents and I~~ will be driving across the country to see the Grand Canyon. ~~My parents and I~~ hope to have a great time.

he/she 3. The new art teacher brought many ideas from the city school where ~~the art teacher~~ worked before.

them 4. Green beans, corn and potatoes are my favorite vegetables. I could eat ~~green beans, corn and potatoes~~ for every meal. I especially like ~~green beans, corn and potatoes~~ in stew.

_it_ 5. I think I left my pen in the library when I was looking up reference materials earlier today. Did you find ~~my pen~~ when you cleaned?

she 6. My grandmother makes very good apple pie. ~~My grandmother~~ said I could learn how to make one the next time we visit.

_us_ 7. My brothers and I could take care of your pets while you are away if you show ~~my brothers and me~~ what you want done.

11

Pronoun Referents

A **pronoun referent** is the noun or nouns a pronoun refers to.

Example:

Green beans, corn and potatoes are my favorite vegetables. I could eat them for every meal.

The pronoun **them** refers to the nouns green beans, corn and potatoes.

Directions: Find the pronoun in each sentence, and write it in the blank below. Underline the word the pronoun refers to. The first one has been done for you.

1. The fruit trees look so beautiful in the spring when they are covered with blossoms.

they

2. Tori is a high school cheerleader. She spends many hours at practice.

she

3. The football must have been slippery because of the rain. The quarterback could not hold on to it.

_it_

4. Aunt Donna needs a babysitter for her three year old tonight.

her

5. The art projects are on the table. Could you please put them on the top shelf along the wall?

them

12

Pronoun Referents

Directions: Find the pronoun in each sentence, and write it in the blank below. Underline the word the pronoun refers to.

1. Did Aaron see the movie _Titanic_? Jay thought it was a very good movie.

_it_

2. Maysie can help you with the spelling words now. Tasha.

you

3. The new tennis coach said to call him after 6:00 tonight.

him

4. Jim, John and Jason called to say they would be later than planned.

they

5. Mrs. Burns enjoyed the cake her class had for the surprise party.

her

6. The children are waiting outside. Ask Josh to take the pinwheels out to them.

them

7. Mrs. Taylor said to go on ahead because she will be late.

she

8. The whole team must sit on the bus until the driver gives us permission to get off.

_us_

9. Dad said the umbrella did a poor job of keeping the rain off him.

him

10. The umbrella was blowing around too much. That's probably why it didn't do a good job.

_it_

13

Pronoun Referents

Directions: Read each sentence carefully. Draw a line to connect each sentence to the correct pronoun.

1. All the teachers in our building said _____ could use a day off!

2. The whole cast spent a lot of time in rehearsals for the school play. _____ should go very well.

3. My Uncle Mike is driving around in a very old car. I know _____ would like to buy a new one.

4. Mr. Barker is having some trouble programming that VCR. Can you help _____?

5. There are too many books on the shelf. I know I can't fit all of _____ into this small box.

6. Ms. Hart slipped on the bleachers at the football game. That's why _____ is using crutches.

him
it
they
she
them
he

14

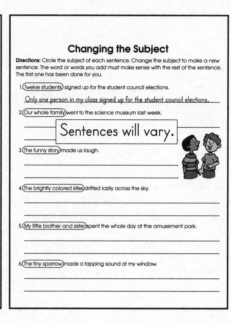

Subjects and Predicates

The **subject** tells who or what the sentence is about. The **predicate** tells what the subject does, did, is doing or will do. A complete sentence must have a subject and a predicate.

Examples:

Subject	Predicate
Sharon	writes to her grandmother every week.
The horse	ran around the track quickly.
My mom's car	is bright green.
Denise	will be here after lunch.

Directions: Circle the subject of each sentence. Underline the predicate.

1. My sister is a very happy person.
2. I wish we had more holidays in the year.
3. Laura is one of the nicest girls in our class.
4. John is fun to have as a friend.
5. The rain nearly ruined our picnic!
6. My birthday present was exactly what I wanted.
7. Your bicycle is parked beside my skateboard.
8. The printer will need to be filled with paper before you use it.
9. Six dogs chased my cat home yesterday!
10. Anthony likes to read anything he can get his hands on.
11. Twelve students signed up for the dance committee.
12. Your teacher seems to be a reasonable person.

15

Changing the Subject

Directions: Circle the subject of each sentence. Change the subject to make a new sentence. The word or words you add must make sense with the rest of the sentence. The first one has been done for you.

1. Twelve students signed up for the student council elections.

Only one person in my class signed up for the student council elections.

2. Our whole family went to the science museum last week.

Sentences will vary.

3. The funny story made us laugh.

4. The brightly colored kites drifted lazily across the sky.

5. My little brother and sister spent the whole day at the amusement park.

6. The tiny sparrow made a tapping sound at my window.

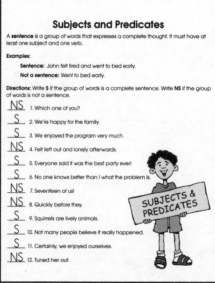

16

Changing the Predicate

Directions: Circle the predicate in each sentence. Change the predicate to make a new sentence. The words you add must make sense with the rest of the sentence. The first one has been done for you.

1. Twelve students signed up for the student council elections.

Twelve students were absent from my class today!

2. Our whole family went to the science museum last week.

Sentences will vary.

3. The funny story made us laugh.

4. The brightly colored kites drifted lazily across the sky.

5. My little brother and sister spent the whole day at the amusement park.

6. The tiny sparrow made a tapping sound at my window.

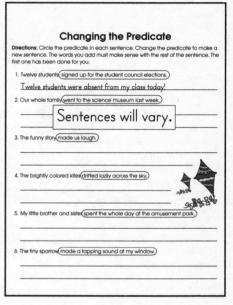

17

Subjects and Predicates

Directions: Write subjects to complete the following sentences.

1. _____ went to school last Wednesday.
2. _____ did not underst____ ____ke.
3. _____ ____ ne could sleep a wink.
4. _____ felt unhappy when the ball game was rained out.
5. _____ wonder what happened at the end of the book.
6. _____ jumped for joy when she won the contest.

Answers will vary.

Directions: Write predicates to complete the following sentences.

7. Everyone _____
8. Dogs _____
9. I _____
10. Justin _____
11. Jokes _____
12. Twelve people _____

Answers will vary.

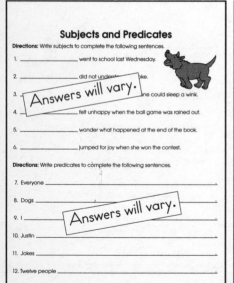

18

Subjects and Predicates

A **sentence** is a group of words that expresses a complete thought. It must have at least one subject and one verb.

Examples:

    Sentence: John felt tired and went to bed early.

    Not a sentence: Went to bed early.

Directions: Write **S** if the group of words is a complete sentence. Write **NS** if the group of words is not a sentence.

NS   1. Which one of you?

S   2. We're happy for the family.

S   3. We enjoyed the program very much.

NS   4. Felt left out and lonely afterwards.

S   5. Everyone said it was the best party ever!

S   6. No one knows better than I what the problem is.

NS   7. Seventeen of us!

NS   8. Quickly before they.

S   9. Squirrels are lively animals.

S   10. Not many people believe it really happened.

S   11. Certainly, we enjoyed ourselves.

NS   12. Tuned her out.

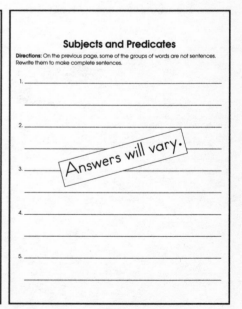

SUBJECTS & PREDICATES

19

Subjects and Predicates

Directions: On the previous page, some of the groups of words are not sentences. Rewrite them to make complete sentences.

1. _____

2. _____

3. _____

Answers will vary.

4. _____

5. _____

20

Compound Subjects

A **compound subject** is a subject with two parts joined by the word **and** or another conjunction. Compound subjects share the same predicate.

Example:

Her shoes were covered with mud. Her ankles were covered with mud, too.
Compound subject: Her shoes and ankles were covered with mud.
The predicate in both sentences is **were covered with mud**.

Directions: Combine each pair of sentences into one sentence with a compound subject.

1. Bill sneezed. Kassie sneezed.
   Bill and Kassie sneezed.

2. Kristin made cookies. Joey made cookies.
   Kristin and Joey made cookies.

3. Fruit flies are insects. Ladybugs are insects.
   Fruit flies and ladybugs are insects.

4. The girls are planning a dance. The boys are planning a dance.
   The girls and boys are planning a dance.

5. Our dog ran after the ducks. Our cat ran after the ducks.
   Our dog and cat ran after the ducks.

6. Joshua got lost in the parking lot. Daniel got lost in the parking lot.
   Joshua and Daniel got lost in the parking lot.

21

Compound Subjects

If sentences do not share the same predicate, they cannot be combined to write a sentence with a compound subject.

Example: Mary laughed at the story.
Tanya laughed at the television show.

Directions: Combine the pairs of sentences that share the same predicate. Write new sentences with compound subjects.

1. Pete loves swimming. Jake loves swimming.
   Pete and Jake love swimming.

2. A bee stung Elizabeth. A hornet stung Elizabeth.
   A bee and a hornet stung Elizabeth.

3. Sharon is smiling. Susan is frowning.

4. The boys have great suntans. The girls have great suntans.
   The boys and girls have great suntans.

5. Six squirrels chased the kitten. Ten dogs chased the kitten.
   Six squirrels and ten dogs chased the kitten.

6. The trees were covered with insects. The roads were covered with ice.

22

Compound Predicates

A **compound predicate** is a predicate with two parts joined by the word **and** or another conjunction. Compound predicates share the same subject.

Example: The baby grabbed the ball. The baby threw the ball.
Compound predicate: The baby grabbed the ball and threw it.
The subject in both sentences is **the baby**.

Directions: Combine each pair of sentences into one sentence to make a compound predicate.

1. Leah jumped on her bike. Leah rode around the block.
   Leah jumped on her bike and rode around the block.

2. Father rolled out the pie crust. Father put the pie crust in the pan.
   Father rolled out the pie crust and put it in the pan.

3. Anthony slipped on the snow. Anthony nearly fell down.
   Anthony slipped on the snow and nearly fell down.

4. My friend lives in a green house. My friend rides a red bicycle.
   My friend lives in a green house and rides a red bicycle.

5. I opened the magazine. I began to read it quietly.
   I opened the magazine and began to read it quietly.

6. My father bought a new plaid shirt. My father wore his new red tie.
   My father bought a new plaid shirt and wore his new red tie.

23

Compound Predicates

Directions: Combine the pairs of sentences that share the same subject. Write new sentences with compound predicates.

1. Jenny picked a bouquet of flowers. Jenny put the flowers in a vase.
   Jenny picked a bouquet of flowers and put them in a vase.

2. I really enjoy ice cream. She really enjoys ice cream.

3. Everyone had a great time at the pep rally. Then everyone went out for a pizza.
   Everyone had a a great time at the pep rally, then went out for pizza.

4. Cassandra built a model airplane. She painted the airplane bright yellow.
   Cassandra built a model airplane and painted it bright yellow.

5. Her brother was really a hard person to get to know. Her sister was very shy, too.

24

Review

Directions: Circle the subjects.

1. (Everyone) felt the day had been a great success.
2. (Christina and Andrea) were both happy to take the day off.
3. (No one) really understood why he was crying.
4. (Mr. Winston, Ms. Fuller and Ms. Landers) took us on a field trip.

Directions: Underline the predicates.

5. Who can tell what will happen tomorrow?
6. Mark was a carpenter by trade and a talented painter, too.
7. The animals yelped and whined in their cages.
8. Airplane rides made her feel sick to her stomach.

Directions: Combine the sentences to make one sentence with a compound subject.

9. Elizabeth ate everything in sight. George ate everything in sight.
   Elizabeth and George ate everything in sight.
10. Wishing something will happen won't make it so. Dreaming something will happen won't make it so.
    Wishing and dreaming something will happen won't make it so.

Directions: Combine the sentences to make one sentence with a compound predicate.

11. I jumped for joy. I hugged all my friends.
    I jumped for joy and hugged all my friends.
12. She ran around the track before the race. She warmed up before the race.
    She ran around the track and warmed up before the race.

25

Intransitive Verbs

An **intransitive verb** is a verb that can stand alone in the predicate because its meaning is complete.

Examples:

He **works**.
They **sleep**.
The dog **ran**.

Other words are not needed after the intransitive verb to make the sentences complete. If more words are added to the sentence, the verbs would still be intransitive because the sentence could stand alone without additional words.

Example:

The noisy concert ended early.
Ended is still an intransitive verb in this sentence.

Directions: Underline the intransitive verb in each sentence.

1. The soccer ball bounced out of bounds.
2. Many autumn leaves fell overnight.
3. Our teacher helped at the band concert yesterday.
4. The small, brown puppy whimpered all night.
5. The school band marched across the field.
6. The cat scratched at the door until dark.
7. The fireworks boomed for hours.
8. The school bus arrived late.
9. A few children cried for their mothers.
10. That feather tickles!
11. Grandfather Wade's barn burned last night.
12. The car tires squealed loudly.
13. The audience laughed at the comedian's jokes.
14. The artist painted in the loft studio.

26

Intransitive Verbs

Directions: Write an intransitive verb after each subject to make a simple sentence.

Answers will vary.

1. He _____
2. Last Wednesday, I _____
3. Every February, they _____
4. Two summers ago, we _____
5. Few people _____
6. Several of us _____
7. The whole class _____
8. No one _____
9. Sixteen dogs _____
10. A harsh rain _____
11. The pony _____
12. Two dozen donuts _____

27

Transitive Verbs

A **transitive verb** needs a direct object to complete its meaning. A **direct object** is the word or words that come after a transitive verb to complete its meaning.

Examples:

Tim **is** taking dance lessons.
He **did** a dance.
The dance **was** a gig.

Is, **did** and **was** are transitive verbs. They must have one or more words after them to complete their meanings.

Example:

The bird **found its nest**.
The words **its nest** are needed after the transitive verb **found** to make the sentence complete.

Directions: Underline the transitive verb in each sentence.

1. The computer <u>made</u> a strange sound.
2. Last night's thunderstorm <u>ruined</u> our sand castles.
3. Aunt Jean <u>raised</u> tomatoes in her garden.
4. Brad <u>accepted</u> the award at the dinner last night.
5. Dad <u>saw</u> us outside his window.
6. The students in Home Economics <u>baked</u> delicious brownies.
7. We <u>had</u> a lot of homework.
8. He will <u>replace</u> the dead battery.
9. Everyone <u>saw</u> the special on television last night.
10. My dog chased <u>the</u> cat.
11. Morgan <u>saw</u> the kites flying high in the sky.
12. We <u>enjoyed</u> the museum trip.

28

Transitive Verbs

Directions: Add a word or words after the transitive verbs to complete the sentences.

Answers will vary.

1. Sylvia threw _____
2. My teacher crossed _____
3. No one polished _____
4. Several students tickled _____
5. The flood destroyed _____
6. The elephant found _____
7. Six days ago we saw _____
8. My favorite book has _____
9. The whole class visited _____
10. My father said _____
11. No one put _____
12. Jessica will repair _____

29

Intransitive and Transitive Verbs

Directions: Write a **T** in the blanks by the sentences that have a transitive verb. Write an **I** in the blanks by the sentences that have an intransitive verb.

I 1. The story was a mystery.
I 2. The people cheered loudly.
I 3. The neighbor's dog barked yesterday.
I 4. We missed her birthday completely.
I 5. The lion roared.
I 6. Together, we sang many songs.
I 7. Elizabeth sharpened her pencil.
I 8. She visited New York City last summer.
I 9. The kitten cried for several hours.
I 10. Gina arrived late for school.
I 11. Did anyone cry when the mayor left?
I 12. The thunder boomed loudly.

30

Intransitive and Transitive Verbs

Directions: Write a **T** in the blanks by the sentences that have a transitive verb. Write an **I** in the blanks by the sentences that have an intransitive verb.

I 1. The whole class saw the video on traffic safety.
I 2. The eagle soared through the evening sky.
I 3. All the monkeys at the zoo chattered noisily.
I 4. We did our homework before supper.
I 5. The school chorus sang all the songs without the piano.
I 6. Mom drew my portrait last summer.
I 7. In gym class, we ran for fifteen minutes!
I 8. Soon, it was dark.
I 9. The bookmobile finally arrived.
I 10. The football game was tied.
I 11. The tiny kitten cried all night long.
I 12. Father drove the van to work today.
I 13. Our principal was at school by 7:00 A.M.
I 14. My sister got a haircut yesterday.

31

Review

Directions: Read the definitions. Then write the correct title on the label of each box, using words from the box.

| transitive verb | subject | compound predicate |
| intransitive verb | predicate | compound subject |

a subject with two parts joined by the word **and** or another conjunction — **compound subject**

the part of the sentence that tells who or what the sentence is about — **subject**

a verb that can stand alone in the predicate because its meaning is complete — **intransitive verb**

a verb that needs a direct object to complete its meaning — **transitive verb**

the part of the sentence that tells what the subject does, did or will do — **predicate**

a predicate with two parts joined by the word **and** or another conjunction — **compound predicate**

32

ENGLISH 4

Verbs: Present, Past and Future Tense

The **present tense** of a verb tells what is happening now.

Examples:

I **am** happy.
I **run** fast.

The **past tense** of a verb tells what has already happened.

Examples:

I **was** happy.
I **ran** fast.

The **future tense** of a verb refers to what is going to happen. The word **will** usually comes before the future tense of a verb.

Examples:

I **will be** happy.
I **will run** fast.

Directions: The sentences below are in the present tense. Rewrite each sentence using the past and future tense of the verb. The first one has been done for you.

1. I think of you as my best friend.
   I thought of you as my best friend.
   I will think of you as my best friend.

2. I hear you coming up the steps.
   I heard you coming up the steps.
   I will hear you coming up the steps.

3. I rush every morning to get ready for school.
   I rushed every morning to get ready for school.
   I will rush every morning to get ready for school.

4. I bake brownies every Saturday.
   I baked brownies every Saturday.
   I will bake brownies every Saturday.

33

Verbs: Present, Past and Future Tense

Directions: Read the following sentences. Write **PRES** if the sentence is in present tense. Write **PAST** if the sentence is in past tense. Write **FUT** if the sentence is in future tense. The first one has been done for you.

FUT 1. I will be thrilled to accept the award.

FUT 2. Will you go with me to the dentist?

PAST 3. I thought he looked familiar!

PAST 4. They ate every single slice of pizza.

PRES 5. I run myself ragged sometimes.

PRES 6. Do you think this project is worthwhile?

PAST 7. No one has been able to repair the broken plate.

PRES 8. Thoughtful gifts are always appreciated.

PAST 9. I like the way he sang!

FUT 10. With a voice like that, he will go a long way.

PRES 11. It's my fondest hope that they visit soon.

PAST 12. I wanted that coat very much.

FUT 13. She'll be happy to take your place.

PRES 14. Everyone thinks the test will be a breeze.

PRES 15. Collecting stamps is her favorite hobby.

34

Adding "ed" to Make Verbs Past Tense

To make many verbs past tense, add **ed**.

Examples:

cook + ed = cooked   wish + ed = wished   play + ed = played

When a verb ends in a **silent e**, drop the **e** and add **ed**.

Examples:

hope + ed = hoped   hate + ed = hated

When a verb ends in **y** after a consonant, change the **y** to **i** and add **ed**.

Examples:

hurry + ed = hurried   marry + ed = married

When a verb ends in a single consonant after a single short vowel, double the final consonant before adding **ed**.

Examples:

stop + ed = stopped   hop + ed = hopped

Directions: Rewrite the present tense of the verb correctly. The first one has been done for you.

1. call	called		11. reply	replied
2. copy	copied		12. top	topped
3. frown	frowned		13. clean	cleaned
4. smile	smiled		14. scream	screamed
5. live	lived		15. clap	clapped
6. talk	talked		16. mop	mopped
7. name	named		17. soap	soaped
8. list	listed		18. choke	choked
9. spy	spied		19. scurry	scurried
10. phone	phoned		20. drop	dropped

35

Verbs With "ed"

Directions: All the sentences below need a **verb + ed**. Write a word from the box to complete each sentence.

talked	watched	served	wagged
picked	shared	typed	washed
knocked	laughed	bothered	

1. She __talked__ on the phone for at least 1 hour.

2. He __washed__ the vegetables while I prepared the broth for the soup.

3. We never __laughed__ as hard as we did at that clown!

4. Each boy in the class __shared__ a story about what he had done over the summer.

5. Father __served__ the popcorn while Mother put the movie in the VCR.

6. I know that noise __bothered__ you last night.

7. The dog's tail __wagged__ so hard it __knocked__ over the picture on the table.

8. Do you know who __picked__ the flowers?

9. She carefully __typed__ her report for health class on the computer.

10. The whole class __watched__ as the rockets shot up into the sky.

36

Irregular Verbs: Past Tense

Irregular verbs change completely in the past tense. Unlike regular verbs, past-tense forms of irregular verbs are not formed by adding **ed**.

Example: The past tense of **go** is **went**.

Other verbs change some letters to form the past tense.

Example: The past tense of **break** is **broke**.

A **helping verb** helps to tell about the past. **Has, have** and **had** are helping verbs used with action verbs to show the action occurred in the past. The past-tense form of the irregular verb sometimes changes when a helping verb is added.

Present Tense Irregular Verb	Past Tense Irregular Verb	Past Tense Irregular Verb With Helper
go	went	have/has/had gone
see	saw	have/has/had seen
do	did	have/has/had done
bring	brought	have/has/had brought
sing	sang	have/has/had sung
drive	drove	have/has/had driven
swim	swam	have/has/had swum
sleep	slept	have/has/had slept

Directions: Choose four words from the chart. Write one sentence using the past-tense form of the verb without a helping verb. Write another sentence using the past-tense form with a helping verb.

1. _____

2. _____

3. _____ Answers will vary.

4. _____

37

The Irregular Verb "Be"

Be is an irregular verb. The present-tense forms of be are **be, am, is** and **are**. The past-tense forms of be are **was** and **were**.

Directions: Write the correct form of **be** in the blanks. The first one has been done for you.

1. I __am__ so happy for you!

2. Jared __was__ unfriendly yesterday.

3. English can __be__ a lot of fun to learn.

4. They __are__ among the nicest people I know.

5. They __were__ late yesterday.

6. She promises she __is__ going to arrive on time.

7. I __am__ nervous right now about the test.

8. If you __are__ satisfied now, so am I.

9. He __was__ as nice to me last week as I had hoped.

10. He can __be__ very gracious.

11. Would you __be__ offended if I moved your desk?

12. He __was__ watching at the window for me yesterday.

38

Page 39

Verbs: "Was" and "Were"

Singular	Plural
I was	we were
you were	you were
he, she, it was	they were

I was over there when it happened

You were?

Directions: Write the correct form of the verb in the blanks. Circle the subject of each sentence. The first one has been done for you.

was 1. (He) was/were so happy that we all smiled, too.

Were 2. Was/Were (you) at the party?

was 3. (She) was/were going to the store.

was 4. (He) was/were always forgetting his hat.

Was 5. Was/Were (she) there?

Were 6. Was/Were (you) sure of your answers?

was 7. (She) was/were glad to help.

were 8. (They) was/were excited.

were 9. Exactly what was/were (you) planning to do?

was 10. (It) was/were wet outside.

were 11. (They) was/were scared by the noise.

Were 12. Was/Were (they) expected before noon?

was 13. (It) was/were too early to get up!

was 14. (She) was/were always early.

were 15. (You) were/was the first person I asked

39

Page 40

Verbs: "Went" and "Gone"

The word **went** is used without a helping verb.

Examples:

Correct: Susan **went** to the store.

Incorrect: Susan **has went** to the store.

Gone is used with a helping verb.

Examples:

Correct: Susan **has gone** to the store.

Incorrect: Susan **gone** to the store.

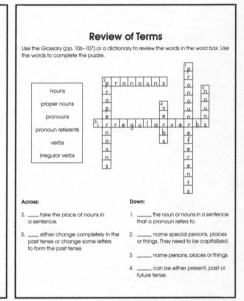

SALE

Directions: Write **C** in the blank if the verb is used correctly. Draw an **X** in the blank if the verb is not used correctly.

_C_ 1. She has gone to my school since last year.

_C_ 2. Has not he been gone a long time?

_X_ 3. He has went to the same class all year.

_X_ 4. I have went to that doctor since I was born.

_C_ 5. She is long gone!

_C_ 6. Who among us has not gone to get a drink yet?

_C_ 7. The class has gone on three field trips this year.

_C_ 8. The class went on three field trips this year.

_X_ 9. Who has not went to the board with the right answer?

_X_ 10. We have not went on our vacation yet.

_X_ 11. Who is went for the pizza?

_C_ 12. The train has been gone for 2 hours.

_C_ 13. The family had gone to the movies.

_X_ 14. Have you went to visit the new bookstore?

_C_ 15. He has gone on and on about how smart you are!

40

Page 41

Review of Terms

Use the Glossary (pp. 106–107) or a dictionary to review the words in the word box. Use the words to complete the puzzle.

Word box:
- nouns
- proper nouns
- pronouns
- pronoun referents
- verbs
- irregular verbs

Crossword (across): 2. pronouns, 5. irregular verbs
Down: 1. pronoun referents, 2. proper nouns, 3. nouns, 4. verbs

Across:

2. _____ take the place of nouns in a sentence.

5. _____ either change completely in the past tense or change some letters to form the past tense.

Down:

1. _____ the noun or nouns in a sentence that a pronoun refers to.

2. _____ name special persons, places or things. They need to be capitalized.

3. _____ name persons, places or things.

4. _____ can be either present, past or future tense.

41

Page 42

Review

Directions: Write **PRES** for present tense, **PAST** for past tense or **FUT** for future tense.

FUT 1. She will help him study.

PAST 2. She helped him study.

PRES 3. She helps him study.

PAST 4. She promised she would help him study.

Directions: Write the past-tense form of these verbs.

cried 5. cry

sighed 6. sigh

hurried 7. hurry

popped 8. pop

Direction: Write the past tense of these irregular verbs with helpers.

9. (go) have _have gone_

10. (sleep) have _have slept_

11. (sing) have _have sung_

12. (see) have _have seen_

Directions: Write the correct form of **be**.

13. They _are_ my closest neighbors.

14. I _was_ very happy for you today.

15. He _was_ there on time yesterday.

16. She _was_ still the nicest girl I know.

Directions: Circle the correct verb.

17. He (went)/gone to my locker.

18. (went)/gone to the beach many times.

19. Have you went/(gone) to this show before?

20. We (went)/gone all the way to the top!

42

Page 43

Direct Objects

A **direct object** is the word or words that come after a transitive verb to complete its meaning. The direct object answers the question **whom** or **what**.

Examples:

Aaron wrote a **letter**.
Letter is the direct object. It tells what Aaron wrote.
We heard **Tom**.
Tom is the direct object. It tells whom we heard.

Directions: Identify the direct object in each sentence. Write it in the blank.

WHOM? WHAT?

_me_ 1. My mother called me.

_it_ 2. The baby dropped it.

mayor 3. I met the mayor.

you 4. I like you!

them 5. No one visited them.

cat 6. We all heard the cat.

stars 7. Jessica saw the stars.

nap 8. She needs a nap.

bone 9. The dog chewed the bone.

doll 10. He hugged the doll.

radio 11. I sold the radio.

banana 12. Douglas ate the banana.

house 13. We finally found the house.

43

Page 44

Direct Objects

Directions: Complete each sentence by writing a direct object.

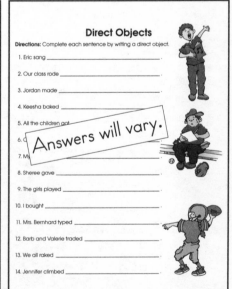

1. Eric sang _____

2. Our class rode _____

3. Jordan made _____

4. Keesha baked _____

5. All the children got _____

6. _____   *Answers will vary.*

7. M_____

8. Sheree gave _____

9. The girls played _____

10. I bought _____

11. Mrs. Bernhard typed _____

12. Barb and Valerie traded _____

13. We all raked _____

14. Jennifer climbed _____

44

Indirect Objects

An **indirect object** is the word or words that come between the verb and the direct object. Indirect objects tells **to whom** or **what** or **for whom** or **what** something is done.

Examples:

He read **me** a funny story.
Me is the indirect object. It tells to whom something (reading a story) was done.
She told her **mother** the truth.
Mother is the indirect object. It tells to whom something (telling the truth) was done.

Directions: Identify the indirect object in each sentence. Write it in the blank.

1. The coach gave Bill a trophy.   Bill
2. He cooked me a wonderful meal.   me
3. She told Maria her secret.   Maria
4. Someone gave my mother a gift.   mother
5. The class gave the principal a new flag for the cafeteria.   principal
6. The restaurant pays the waiter a good salary.   waiter
7. You should tell your dad the truth.   dad
8. She sent her son a plane ticket.   son
9. The waiter served the patron a salad.   patron
10. Grandma gave the baby a kiss.   baby
11. I sold Steve some cookies.   Steve
12. He told us six jokes.   us
13. She brought the boy a sucker.   boy

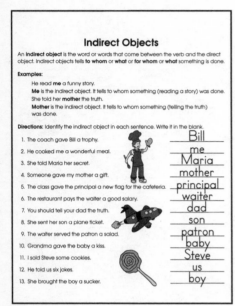

45

Indirect Objects

Directions: Use the words below to complete each sentence with an indirect object. The first one has been done for you.

a. the librarian	b. the coach	c. all the teachers	d. the class
e. Mom	f. the waiter	g. all of us	h. our parents

c 1. The principal gave (___) the n... about the meeting.

Sample answers:

e 2. My sister told (___) the truth.

d 3. Our teacher told (___) the homework assignment.

g 4. Dad bought (___) a delicious treat.

a 5. She gave (___) her overdue books.

h 6. We helped (___) clean the house.

f 7. The customer gave (___) a good tip.

b 8. Michael told (___) about his sore leg.

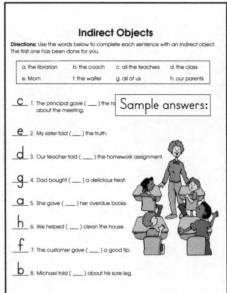

46

Direct and Indirect Objects

Example: Sharon told Jennifer a funny (story.)

Jennifer is the indirect object. It tells **to whom** Sharon told the story. Story is the direct object. It tells **what** Sharon told.

Directions: Circle the direct object in each sentence. Underline the indirect object.

1. The teacher gave the class a (test.)
2. Josh brought Elizabeth the (book.)
3. Someone left the cat a (present.)
4. The poet read David all his (poems.)
5. My big brother handed me the (ticket.)
6. Luke told everyone the (secret.)
7. Jason handed his dad the (newspaper.)
8. Mother bought Jack a (suitcase.)
9. They cooked us an excellent (dinner.)
10. I loaned Jonathan my (bike.)
11. She threw him a curve (ball.)
12. You tell Dad the (truth!)

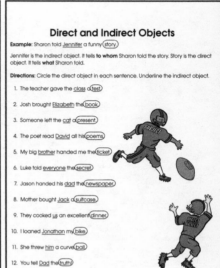

47

Direct and Indirect Objects

Directions: Add a direct object and an indirect object to each sentence. Circle the direct objects and underline the indirect objects.

1. The happy clown gave _____
2. The smiling politician offered _____
3. My big brother handed _____
4. His uncle Seth works _____
5. The friendly waiter gave _____
6. Elizabeth told _____
7. My mother broug... _____
8. He served _____
9. Jane should tell _____
10. Someone threw _____
11. The bookstore sent _____
12. The salesclerk gave _____
13. The magician brought _____
14. Her father cooked _____
15. His boss pays _____

Answers will vary.

48

More Direct and Indirect Objects

Directions: Write the direct and indirect objects in the blanks below.

1. All the girls wrote letters to their friends.
2. Each child brought the teacher an apple.
3. My Dad gave my Mom flowers on their anniversary.
4. Christopher gave the class a book report.
5. The bus drivers gave the children oranges.
6. We showed Mom the prizes.
7. My brother gave Mom and Dad his report card.

	Direct Objects	Indirect Objects
1.	letters	friends
2.	apple	teacher
3.	flowers	Mom
4.	report	class
5.	oranges	children
6.	prizes	Mom
7.	card	Mom, Dad

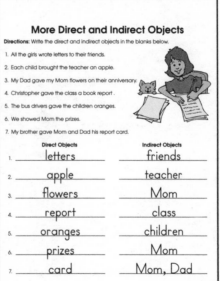

49

Review

Directions: Identify transitive and intransitive verbs by writing a **T** or an **I** in each blank.

I 1. The football game was exciting.
T 2. No one believed her story.
I 3. My friend's cat meowed when I picked it up.
I 4. A heavy rain fell.
I 5. The baby cried and cried!
T 6. Jason polished his shoes.
T 7. Michael set the table.
I 8. Everyone cheered.

Directions: Write the direct objects in the blanks.

eggs 9. My father dropped the eggs.
us 10. No one could find us.
peas 11. Jessica likes peas.
light 12. We finally saw the light.

Directions: Write the indirect objects in the blanks.

me 13. My father handed me the eggs.
John 14. Anthony told John the joke.
him 15. I passed him the jelly beans.
us 16. They gave us the raincoats.

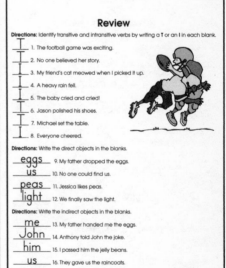

50

Adverbs

Adverbs are words that tell when, where or how.

Adverbs of time tell when.

Example:

The train left yesterday.

Yesterday is an adverb of time. It tells when the train left.

Adverbs of place tell where.

Example:

The girl walked away.

Away is an adverb of place. It tells where the girl walked.

Adverbs of manner tell how.

Example:

The boy walked quickly.

Quickly is an adverb of manner. It tells how the boy walked.

Directions: Write the adverb for each sentence in the first blank. In the second blank, write whether it is an adverb of time, place or manner. The first one has been done for you.

1. The family ate downstairs.	downstairs	place
2. The relatives laughed loudly.	loudly	manner
3. We will finish tomorrow.	tomorrow	time
4. The snowstorm will stop soon.	soon	time
5. She sings beautifully!	beautifully	manner
6. The baby slept soundly.	soundly	manner
7. The elevator stopped suddenly.	suddenly	manner
8. Does the plane leave today?	today	time
9. The phone call came yesterday.	yesterday	time
10. She ran outside.	outside	place

51

Adverbs of Time

Directions: Choose a word or group of words from the box to complete each sentence. Make sure the adverb you choose makes sense with the rest of the sentence.

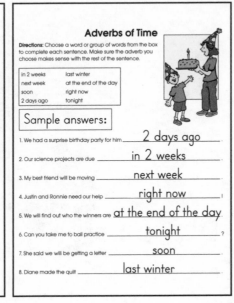

in 2 weeks	last winter
next week	at the end of the day
soon	right now
2 days ago	tonight

Sample answers:

1. We had a surprise birthday party for him ___ 2 days ago
2. Our science projects are due ___ in 2 weeks
3. My best friend will be moving ___ next week
4. Justin and Ronnie need our help ___ right now ___ !
5. We will find out who the winners are ___ at the end of the day.
6. Can you take me to ball practice ___ tonight ___ ?
7. She said we will be getting a letter ___ soon
8. Diane made the quilt ___ last winter

52

Adverbs of Place

Directions: Choose one word from the box to complete each sentence. Make sure the adverb you choose makes sense with the rest of the sentence.

inside	upstairs	below	everywhere
home	somewhere	outside	there

Sample answers:

1. Each child took a new library book ___ home
2. We looked ___ everywhere ___ for his jacket.
3. We will have recess ___ inside ___ because it is raining.
4. From the top of the mountain we could see the village far ___ below
5. My sister and I share a bedroom ___ upstairs
6. The teacher warned the children, "You must play with the ball ___ outside ___ ."
7. Mother said, "I know that recipe is ___ somewhere ___ in this file box!"
8. You can put the chair ___ there

53

Adverbs of Manner

Directions: Choose a word from the box to complete each sentence. Make sure the adverb you choose makes sense with the rest of the sentence. One word will be used twice.

quickly	carefully	loudly	easily	carelessly	slowly

Sample answers:

1. The scouts crossed the old bridge ___ carefully
2. We watched the turtle move ___ slowly ___ across the yard.
3. Everyone completed the math test ___ quickly
4. The quarterback scampered ___ easily ___ down the sideline.
5. The mother ___ carefully ___ cleaned the child's sore knee.
6. The fire was caused by someone ___ carelessly ___ tossing a match.
7. The alarm rang ___ loudly ___ while we were eating.

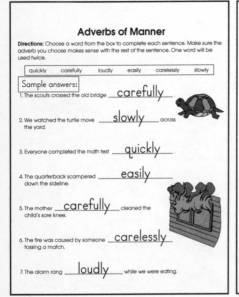

54

Adjectives That Add "er"

The suffix **er** is often added to adjectives to compare two things.

Example:

My feet are **large**.

Your feet are **larger** than my feet.

When a one-syllable adjective ends in a single consonant and the vowel is short, double the final consonant before adding **er**. When a word ends in two or more consonants, add **er**.

Examples:

big — bigger (single consonant)

bold — bolder (two consonants)

When an adjective ends in **y**, change the **y** to **i** before adding **er**.

Examples:

easy — easier

greasy — greasier

breezy — breezier

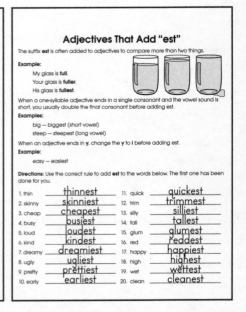

Directions: Use the correct rule to add **er** to the words below. The first one has been done for you.

1. fast	faster	11. skinny	skinnier
2. thin	thinner	12. fat	fatter
3. long	longer	13. poor	poorer
4. few	fewer	14. juicy	juicier
5. ugly	uglier	15. early	earlier
6. silly	sillier	16. clean	cleaner
7. busy	busier	17. thick	thicker
8. grand	grander	18. creamy	creamier
9. lean	leaner	19. deep	deeper
10. young	younger	20. lazy	lazier

55

Adjectives That Add "est"

The suffix **est** is often added to adjectives to compare more than two things.

Example:

My glass is **full**.

Your glass is **fuller**.

His glass is **fullest**.

When a one-syllable adjective ends in a single consonant and the vowel sound is short, you usually double the final consonant before adding **est**.

Examples:

big — biggest (short vowel)

steep — steepest (long vowel)

When an adjective ends in **y**, change the **y** to **i** before adding **est**.

Example:

easy — easiest

Directions: Use the correct rule to add **est** to the words below. The first one has been done for you.

1. thin	thinnest	11. quick	quickest
2. skinny	skinniest	12. trim	trimmest
3. cheap	cheapest	13. silly	silliest
4. busy	busiest	14. tall	tallest
5. loud	loudest	15. glum	glumest
6. kind	kindest	16. red	reddest
7. dreamy	dreamiest	17. happy	happiest
8. ugly	ugliest	18. high	highest
9. pretty	prettiest	19. wet	wettest
10. early	earliest	20. clean	cleanest

56

Adding "er" and "est" to Adjectives

Directions: Circle the correct adjective for each sentence. The first one has been done for you.

1. Of all the students in the gym, her voice was (louder, **loudest**).

2. "I can tell you are (**busier**, busiest) than I am," he said to the librarian.

3. If you and Carl stand back to back, I can see which one is (**taller**, tallest).

4. She is the (kinder, **kindest**) teacher in the whole building.

5. Wow! That is the (bigger, **biggest**) pumpkin I have ever seen!

6. I believe your flashlight is (**brighter**, brightest) than mine.

7. "This is the (cleaner, **cleanest**) your room has been in a long time," Mother said.

8. The leaves on that plant are (**prettier**, prettiest) than the ones on the window sill.

57

Adjectives Preceded by "More"

Most adjectives of two or more syllables are preceded by the word **more** as a way to show comparison between two things.

Examples:
Correct: intelligent, more intelligent
Incorrect: intelligenter
Correct: famous, more famous
Incorrect: famouser

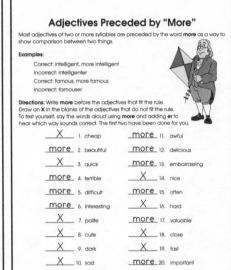

Directions: Write **more** before the adjectives that fit the rule. Draw an **X** in the blanks of the adjectives that do not fit the rule. To test yourself, say the words aloud using **more** and adding **er** to hear which way sounds correct. The first two have been done for you.

__X__	1. cheap	__more__	11. awful
__more__	2. beautiful	__more__	12. delicious
__X__	3. quick	__more__	13. embarrassing
__more__	4. terrible	__X__	14. nice
__more__	5. difficult	__more__	15. often
__more__	6. interesting	__X__	16. hard
__X__	7. polite	__more__	17. valuable
__X__	8. cute	__X__	18. close
__X__	9. dark	__X__	19. fast
__X__	10. sad	__more__	20. important

58

Adjectives Using "er" or "More"

Directions: Add the word or words needed in each sentence. The first one has been done for you.

1. I thought the book was **more interesting** than the movie. (interesting)

2. Do you want to carry this box? It is ___**lighter**___ than the one you have now. (light)

3. I noticed you are moving ___**slower**___ this morning. Does your ankle still bother you? (slow)

4. Thomas Edison is probably ___**more famous**___ for his invention of the electric light bulb than of the phonograph. (famous)

5. She stuck out her lower lip and whined, "Your ice-cream cone is ___**bigger**___ than mine!" (big)

6. Mom said my room was ___**cleaner**___ than it has been in a long time. (clean)

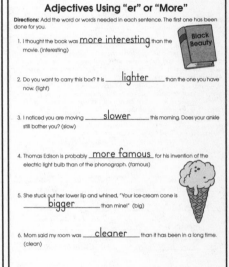

59

Adjectives Preceded by "Most"

Most adjectives of two or more syllables are preceded by the word **most** as a way to show comparison between more than two things.

Examples:
Correct: intelligent, most intelligent
Incorrect: intelligentest
Correct: famous, most famous
Incorrect: famousest

Directions: Read the following groups of sentences. In the last sentence for each group, write the adjective preceded by **most**. The first one has been done for you.

1. My uncle is intelligent.
My aunt is more intelligent.
My cousin is the ___most intelligent___.

2. I am thankful.
My brother is more thankful.
My parents are the ___most thankful___.

3. Your sister is polite.
Your brother is more polite.
You are the ___most polite___.

4. The blouse was expensive.
The sweater was more expensive.
The coat was the ___most expensive___.

5. The class was fortunate.
The teacher was more fortunate.
The principal was the ___most fortunate___.

6. The cookies were delicious.
The cake was even more delicious.
The brownies were the ___most delicious___.

7. That painting is elaborate.
The sculpture is more elaborate.
The finger painting is the ___most elaborate___.

60

Adjectives Using "est" or "Most"

Directions: Add the word or words needed to complete each sentence. The first one has been done for you.

1. The star over there is the ___**brightest**___ of all! (bright)

2. "I believe this is the ___**most delightful**___ time I have ever had," said Mackenzie. (delightful)

3. That game was the ___**most exciting**___ one of the whole year! (exciting)

4. I think this tree has the ___**greenest**___ leaves. (green)

5. We will need the ___**sharpest**___ knife you have to cut the face for the jack-o-lantern. (sharp)

6. Everyone agreed that your chocolate chip cookies were the ___**most delicious**___ of all. (delicious)

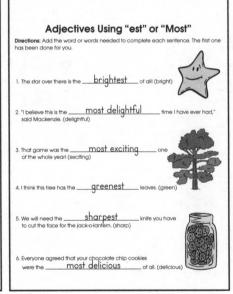

61

Adjectives and Adverbs

Directions: Write **ADJ** on the line if the bold word is an adjective. Write **ADV** if the bold word is an adverb. The first one has been done for you.

__ADV__	1. That road leads **nowhere**.
__ADJ__	2. The squirrel was **nearby**.
__ADJ__	3. Her **delicious** cookies were all eaten.
__ADV__	4. Everyone rushed **indoors**.
__ADV__	5. He **quickly** zipped his jacket.
__ADJ__	6. She hummed a **popular** tune.
__ADJ__	7. Her **sunny** smile warmed my heart.
__ADV__	8. I hung your coat **there**.
__ADV__	9. Bring that **here** this minute!
__ADV__	10. We all walked **back** to school.
__ADJ__	11. The **skinniest** boy ate the most food!
__ADJ__	12. She acts like a **famous** person.
__ADJ__	13. The **silliest** jokes always make me laugh.
__ADV__	14. She must have parked her car **somewhere**!
__ADV__	15. Did you take the test **today**?

62

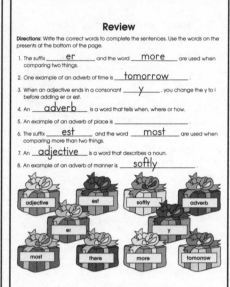

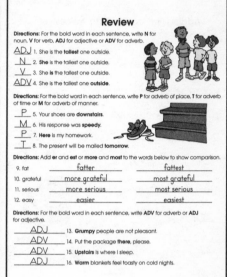

Panel 63

Adjectives and Adverbs

Directions: Read this story. Underline the adjectives. Circle the adverbs. Write the words in the correct column at the end of the story.

Surprise!

Emily and Elizabeth tiptoed quietly through the dark hallway. Even though none of the lights were lit, they knew the presents were there. Every year the two sisters had gone to Mom and Dad's bedroom to wake them on Christmas morning. This year would be different, they decided.

Last night after supper, they had secretly plotted to look early in the morning before Mom and Dad were awake. The girls knew that Emily's red-and-green stocking and Elizabeth's striped stocking hung by the brick fireplace. They knew the beautiful tree was in the corner by the rocking chair.

"Won't Mom and Dad be surprised to awaken on their own?" asked Elizabeth quietly.

Emily whispered, "Click the overhead lights so we can see better."

"You don't have to whisper," said a voice.

There sat Mom and Dad as the Christmas-tree lights suddenly shone.

Dad said, "I guess the surprise is on you two!"

Answers may include:

Adverbs	Adjectives	
quietly	dark	striped
there	none	brick
secretly	every	beautiful
early	two	rocking
quietly	this	Christmas-tree
better	last	
suddenly	different	
	red-and-green	

63

Panel 64

Review

Directions: Write the correct words to complete the sentences. Use the words on the presents at the bottom of the page.

1. The suffix ____er____ and the word ___more___ are used when comparing two things.

2. One example of an adverb of time is ___tomorrow___.

3. When an adjective ends in a consonant ___y___, you change the y to i before adding er or est.

4. An ___adverb___ is a word that tells when, where or how.

5. An example of an adverb of place is _____.

6. The suffix ___est___ and the word ___most___ are used when comparing more than two things.

7. An ___adjective___ is a word that describes a noun.

8. An example of an adverb of manner is ___softly___.

Presents: adjective, est, softly, adverb, er, y, most, there, more, tomorrow

64

Panel 65

Review

Directions: For the bold word in each sentence, write N for noun, V for verb, ADJ for adjective or ADV for adverb.

ADJ 1. She is the **tallest** one outside.

N 2. **She** is the tallest one outside.

V 3. She **is** the tallest one outside.

ADV 4. She is the tallest one **outside**.

Directions: For the bold word in each sentence, write P for adverb of place, T for adverb of time or M for adverb of manner.

P 5. Your shoes are **downstairs**.

M 6. His response was **speedy**.

P 7. **Here** is my homework.

T 8. The present will be mailed **tomorrow**.

Directions: Add **er** and **est** or **more** and **most** to the words below to show comparison.

9. fat	fatter	fattest
10. grateful	more grateful	most grateful
11. serious	more serious	most serious
12. easy	easier	easiest

Directions: For the bold word in each sentence, write ADV for adverb or ADJ for adjective.

ADJ 13. **Grumpy** people are not pleasant.

ADV 14. Put the package **there**, please.

ADV 15. **Upstairs** is where I sleep.

ADJ 16. **Warm** blankets feel toasty on cold nights.

65

Panel 66

"Good" and "Well"

Use the word **good** to describe a noun. Good is an adjective.

Example: She is a **good** teacher.

Use the word **well** to tell or ask how something is done or to describe someone's health. Well is an adverb. It describes a verb.

Example: She is not feeling **well**.

Directions: Write **good** or **well** in the blanks to complete the sentences correctly. The first one has been done for you.

good 1. Our team could use a good/well captain.
well 2. The puny kitten doesn't look good/well.
well 3. He did his job so good/well that everyone praised him.
good 4. Whining isn't a good/well habit.
well 5. I might just as good/well do it myself.
well 6. She was one of the most well-/good- liked girls at school.
well 7. I did the book report as good/well as I could.
well 8. The television works very good/well.
good 9. You did a good/well job repairing the TV!
well 10. Thanks for a job good/well done!
good 11. You did a good/well job fixing the computer.
well 12. You had better treat your friends good/well.
well 13. Can your grandmother hear good/well?
well 14. Your brother will be well/good soon.

66

Panel 67

"Your" and "You're"

The word **your** shows possession.

Examples:
Is that **your** book?
I visited **your** class.

The word **you're** is a contraction for **you are**. A **contraction** is two words joined together as one. An apostrophe shows where letters have been left out.

Examples:
You're doing well on that painting.
If **you're** going to pass the test, you should study.

Directions: Write **your** or **you're** on the blanks to complete the sentences correctly. The first one has been done for you.

You're 1. Your/You're the best friend I have!
You're 2. Your/You're going to drop that!
Your 3. Your/You're brother came to see me.
your 4. Is that your/you're cat?
you're 5. If your/you're going, you'd better hurry!
your 6. Why are your/you're fingers so red?
your 7. It's none of your/you're business!
Your 8. Your/You're bike's front tire is low.
You're 9. Your/You're kidding!
your 10. Have it your/you're way.
your 11. I thought your/you're report was great!
you're 12. He thinks your/you're wonderful!
your 13. What is your/you're first choice?
your 14. What's your/you're opinion?
you're 15. If your/you're going, so am I!
You're 16. Your/You're welcome.

67

Panel 68

"Good" and "Well"; "Your" and "You're"

Directions: Choose the correct word for each sentence: good, well, your or you're.

1. "I was quite pleased with the ___good___ job you did on the report," said Mr. Free.

2. Our teacher said to make sure you take ___your___ jacket along on the trip.

3. My mother makes really ___good___ potato soup. You will enjoy lunch today!

4. Are you sure ___you're___ going to be ready for the math test tomorrow?

5. We have a substitute teacher because Ms. Stigall doesn't feel ___well___ this afternoon.

6. Coach Jennings said that you must have ___your___ health card signed before you can play basketball.

68

"Good" and "Well"; "Your" and "You're"

Directions: Choose the correct word for each sentence: **good, well, your** or **you're.**

1. Are you sure you can see ___well___ enough to read with the lighting you have?

2. ___You're___ going to need a paint smock when you go to art class tomorrow afternoon.

3. I can see ___you're___ having some trouble. Can I help with that?

4. The music department needs to buy a speaker system that has ___good___ quality sound.

5. The principal asked, "Where is ___your___ hall pass?"

6. You must do the job ___well___ if you expect to keep it.

7. The traffic policeman said, "May I please see ___your___ driver's license?"

8. The story you wrote for English class was done quite ___well___.

9. That radio station you listen to is a ___good___ one.

10. Let us know if ___you're___ unable to attend the meeting on Saturday.

69

"Its" and "It's"

The word **its** shows ownership.

Examples:

Its leaves have all turned green.
Its paw was injured.

The word **It's** is a contraction for **it is.**

Examples:

It's better to be early than late.
It's not fair!

Directions: Write **its** or **it's** to complete the sentences correctly. The first one has been done for you.

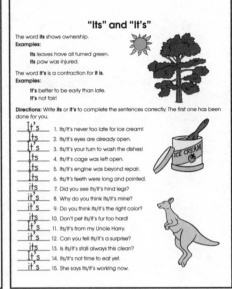

___It's___ 1. Its/It's never too late for ice cream!
___Its___ 2. Its/It's eyes are already open.
___Its___ 3. Its/It's your turn to wash the dishes!
___Its___ 4. Its/It's cage was left open.
___Its___ 5. Its/It's engine was beyond repair.
___Its___ 6. Its/It's teeth were long and pointed.
___its___ 7. Did you see its/it's hind legs?
___it's___ 8. Why do you think its/it's mine?
___it's___ 9. Do you think its/it's the right color?
___its___ 10. Don't pet its/it's fur too hard!
___It's___ 11. Its/It's from my Uncle Harry.
___it's___ 12. Can you tell its/it's a surprise?
___its___ 13. Is its/it's stall always this clean?
___It's___ 14. Its/It's not time to eat yet.
___it's___ 15. She says its/it's working now.

70

"Can" and "May"

The word **can** means am able to or to be able to.

Examples:

I **can** do that for you.
Can you do that for me?

The word **may** means be allowed to or permitted to. May is used to ask or give permission. **May** can also mean **might** or **perhaps.**

Examples:

May I be excused?
You **may** sit here.

Directions: Write **can** or **may** on the blanks to complete the sentences correctly. The first one has been done for you.

___May___ 1. Can/May I help you?
___can___ 2. He's smart. He can/may do it himself.
___may___ 3. When can/may I have my dessert?
___can___ 4. I can/may tell you exactly what she said.
___can___ 5. He can/may speak French fluently.
___may___ 6. You can/may use my pencil.
___may___ 7. I can/may be allowed to attend the concert.
___can___ 8. It's bright. I can/may see you!
___May___ 9. Can/May my friend stay for dinner?
___may___ 10. You can/may leave when your report is finished.
___can___ 11. I can/may see your point!
___can___ 12. She can/may dance well.
___Can___ 13. Can/May you hear the dog barking?
___Can___ 14. Can/May you help me button this sweater?
___may___ 15. Mother, can/may I go to the movies?

71

"Its" and "It's"; "Can" and "May"

Directions: Choose the correct word for each sentence: **its, it's, can** or **may.**

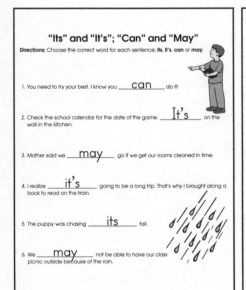

1. You need to try your best. I know you ___can___ do it!

2. Check the school calendar for the date of the game. ___It's___ on the wall in the kitchen.

3. Mother said we ___may___ go if we get our rooms cleaned in time.

4. I realize ___it's___ going to be a long trip. That's why I brought along a book to read on the train.

5. The puppy was chasing ___its___ tail.

6. We ___may___ not be able to have our class picnic outside because of the rain.

72

"Its" and "It's"; "Can" and "May"

Directions: Choose the correct word for each sentence: **its, it's, can** or **may.**

1. "It looks as though your arms are full, Diane. ___May___ I help you with some of those things?" asked Michele.

2. The squirrel ___can___ climb up the tree quickly with his mouth full of acorns.

3. She has had her school jacket so long that it is beginning to lose ___its___ color.

4. How many laps around the track ___can___ you do?

5. Sometimes you can tell what a story is going to be about by looking at ___its___ title.

6. Our house ___may___ need to be painted again in two or three years.

7. Mother asked, "Jon, ___can___ you open the door for your father?"

8. ___It's___ going to be a while until your birthday, but do you know what you want?

9. I can feel it in the air: ___it's___ going to snow soon.

10. If I'm careful with it, ___may___ I borrow your CD player?

73

"Sit" and "Set"

The word **sit** means to rest.

Examples:

Please **sit** here!
Will you **sit** by me?

The word **set** means to put or place something.

Examples:

Set your purse there.
Set the dishes on the table.

Directions: Write **sit** or **set** to complete the sentences correctly. The first one has been done for you.

___sit___ 1. Would you please sit/set down here?
___set___ 2. You can sit/set the groceries there.
___set___ 3. She sit/set her suitcase in the closet.
___set___ 4. He sit/set his watch for half past three.
___sit___ 5. She's a person who can't sit/set still.
___set___ 6. Sit/Set the baby on the couch beside me.
___set___ 7. Where did you sit/set your new shoes?
___sit___ 8. They decided to sit/set together during the movie.
___sit___ 9. Let me sit/set you straight on that!
___sit___ 10. Instead of swimming, he decided to sit/set in the water.
___set___ 11. He sit/set the greasy pan in the sink.
___set___ 12. She sit/set the file folder on her desk.
___sit___ 13. Don't ever sit/set on the refrigerator!
___set___ 14. She sit/set the candles on the cake.
___set___ 15. Get ready! Get sit/set! Go!

74

"They're," "Their," "There"

The word **they're** is a contraction for **they are**.

Examples:

They're our very best friends!

Ask them if **they're** coming over tomorrow.

The word **their** shows ownership.

Examples:

Their dog is friendly.

It's **their** bicycle.

The word **there** shows place or direction.

Examples:

Look over **there**.

There it is.

Directions: Write **they're**, **their** or **there** to complete the sentences correctly. The first one has been done for you.

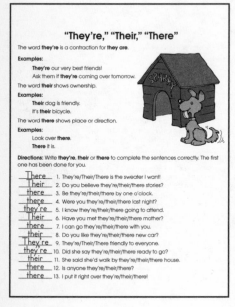

There   1. They're/Their/There is the sweater I want!
Their   2. Do you believe they're/their/there stories?
there   3. Be they're/their/there by one o'clock.
there   4. Were you they're/their/there last night?
they're 5. I know they're/their/there going to attend.
Their   6. Have you met they're/their/there mother?
there   7. I can go they're/their/there with you.
their   8. Do you like they're/their/there new car?
They're 9. They're/Their/There friendly to everyone.
they're 10. Did she say they're/their/there ready to go?
their   11. She said she'd walk by they're/their/there house.
there   12. Is anyone they're/their/there?
there   13. I put it right over they're/their/there!

75

"Sit" and "Set"; "They're," "There," "Their"

Directions: Choose the correct word for each sentence: **sit**, **set**, **they're**, **there** or **their**.

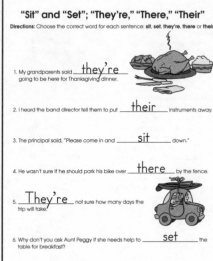

1. My grandparents said __they're__ going to be here for Thanksgiving dinner.

2. I heard the band director tell them to put __their__ instruments away.

3. The principal said, "Please come in and __sit__ down."

4. He wasn't sure if he should park his bike over __there__ by the fence.

5. __They're__ not sure how many days the trip will take.

6. Why don't you ask Aunt Peggy if she needs help to __set__ the table for breakfast?

76

"Sit" and "Set"; "They're," "There," "Their"

Directions: Choose the correct word for each sentence: **sit**, **set**, **they're**, **there** or **their**.

1. Her muscles became tense as she heard the gym teacher say, "Get ready, get __set__, go!"

2. When we choose our seats on the bus will you __sit__ with me?

3. __There__ is my library book! I wondered where I had left it!

4. My little brother and his friend said __they're__ not going to the ball game with us.

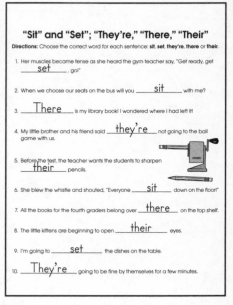

5. Before the test, the teacher wants the students to sharpen __their__ pencils.

6. She blew the whistle and shouted, "Everyone __sit__ down on the floor!"

7. All the books for the fourth graders belong over __there__ on the top shelf.

8. The little kittens are beginning to open __their__ eyes.

9. I'm going to __set__ the dishes on the table.

10. __They're__ going to be fine by themselves for a few minutes.

77

"This" and "These"

The word **this** is an adjective that refers to things that are near. **This** always describes a singular noun. Singular means one.

Example:

I'll buy **this** coat.

(Coat is singular.)

The word **these** is also an adjective that refers to things that are near. **These** always describes a plural noun. A plural refers to more than one thing.

Example:

I will buy **these** flowers.

(Flowers is a plural noun.)

Directions: Write **this** or **these** to complete the sentences correctly. The first one has been done for you.

these   1. I will take this/these cookies with me.
these   2. Do you want this/these seeds?
these   3. Did you try this/these nuts?
this   4. Do it this/these way!
this   5. What do you know about this/these situation?
these   6. Did you open this/these doors?
this   7. Did you open this/these window?
this   8. What is the meaning of this/these letters?
these   9. Will you carry this/these books for me?
These   10. This/These pans are hot!
this   11. Do you think this/these light is too bright?
these   12. Are this/these boots yours?
this   13. Do you like this/these rainy weather?

78

Review

Directions: Complete the sentences by writing the correct words in the blanks.

good   1. You have a good/well attitude.
well   2. The teacher was not feeling good/well.
good   3. She sang extremely good/well.
good   4. Everyone said Josh was a good/well boy.
You're   5. Your/You're going to be sorry for that!
you're   6. Tell her your/you're serious.
Your   7. Your/You're report was wonderful!
You're   8. Your/You're the best person for the job.
it's   9. Do you think its/it's going to have babies?
Its   10. Its/It's back paw had a thorn in it.
It's   11. Its/It's fun to make new friends.
its   12. Is its/it's mother always nearby?
may   13. How can/may I help you?
may   14. You can/may come in now.
Can   15. Can/May you lift this for me?
can   16. She can/may sing soprano.
sit   17. I'll wait for you to sit/set down first.
set   18. We sit/set our dirty boots outside.
their   19. It's they're/their/there turn to choose.
There   20. They're/Their/There is your answer!
they're 21. They say they're/their/there coming.
this   22. I must have this/these one!
these   23. I saw this/these gloves at the store.
these   24. He said this/these were his.

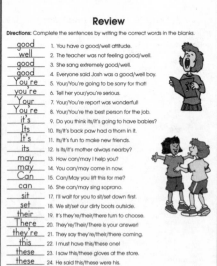

79

Review

Directions: Write the correct answers in the blanks using the words in the box.

good	well	your	you're	its
it's	can	may	sit	set
they're	there	their	this	these

1. __this__ is an adjective that refers to a particular thing.

2. Use __well__ to tell or ask how something is done or to describe someone's health.

3. __It's__ is a contraction for It is.

4. __these__ describes a plural noun and refers to particular things.

5. __sit__ means to rest.

6. __can__ means am able to or to be able to.

7. __they're__ is a contraction for they are.

8. __your__ __its__ and __their__ show ownership or possession.

9. Use __may__ to ask politely to be permitted to do something.

10. __you're__ is a contraction for you are.

11. __set__ means to place or put.

12. __good__ describes a noun.

13. Use __there__ to show direction or placement.

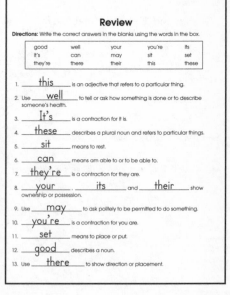

80

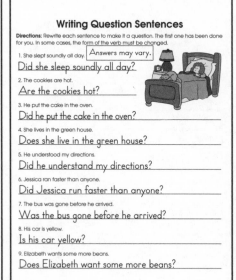

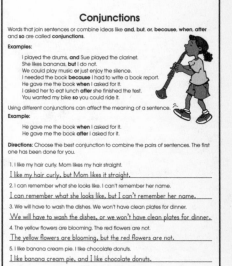

Making Sense of Sentences

A **statement** is a sentence that tells something. It ends with a period (.).

Example: Columbus is the capital of Ohio.

A **question** is a sentence that asks something. It ends with a question mark (?).

Example: Do you like waffles?

An **exclamation** is a sentence that shows strong feeling. It ends with an exclamation mark (!).

Example: You're the best friend in the world!

A **command** is a sentence that orders someone to do something. It ends with a period or exclamation mark.

Example: Shut the door. Watch out for that trunk!

A **request** is a sentence that asks someone to do something. It ends with a period or question mark.

Example: Please shut the door. | Answers may vary but could include: |

Directions: Write **S** if the sentence makes a statement, **Q** if it asks a question, **E** if it is an exclamation, **C** if it issues a command or **R** if it makes a request. Punctuate each sentence correctly.

R 1. Please open your mouth.
Q 2. Will you be going to the party?
E 3. That's hot!
C 4. Give me the car keys right now.
Q 5. Do you think she will run fast?
S 6. It's cold today.
S 7. You're incredible.
E 8. Run for your life!
Q 9. Is today the deadline?
S 10. I turned in my paper early.

C 11. Call the doctor immediately.
C 12. Turn around and touch your toes.
Q 13. Be at my house at noon tomorrow.
Q 14. Give me a clue.
Q 15. Can you give me a clue?
R 16. Please wipe your face.
S 17. It's time for me to go home.
S 18. No one believed what she said.
Q 19. Are you interested?
S 20. He's badly hurt.

81

Writing Question Sentences

Directions: Rewrite each sentence to make it a question. The first one has been done for you. In some cases, the form of the verb must be changed.

1. She slept soundly all day. | Answers may vary. |

Did she sleep soundly all day?

2. The cookies are hot.

Are the cookies hot?

3. He put the cake in the oven.

Did he put the cake in the oven?

4. She lives in the green house.

Does she live in the green house?

5. He understood my directions.

Did he understand my directions?

6. Jessica ran faster than anyone.

Did Jessica run faster than anyone?

7. The bus was gone before he arrived.

Was the bus gone before he arrived?

8. His car is yellow.

Is his car yellow?

9. Elizabeth wants some more beans.

Does Elizabeth want some more beans?

82

Conjunctions

Words that join sentences or combine ideas like **and**, **but**, **or**, **because**, **when**, **after** and **so** are called **conjunctions**.

Examples:

I played the drums, **and** Sue played the clarinet.
She likes bananas, **but** I do not.
We could play music **or** just enjoy the silence.
I needed the book **because** I had to write a book report.
He gave me the book **when** I asked for it.
I asked her to eat lunch **after** she finished the test.
You wanted my bike **so** you could ride it.

Using different conjunctions can affect the meaning of a sentence.

Example:

He gave me the book **when** I asked for it.
He gave me the book **after** I asked for it.

Directions: Choose the best conjunction to combine the pairs of sentences. The first one has been done for you.

1. I like my hair curly. Mom likes my hair straight.
I like my hair curly, but Mom likes it straight.

2. I can remember what she looks like. I can't remember her name.
I can remember what she looks like, but I can't remember her name.

3. We will have to wash the dishes. We won't have clean plates for dinner.
We will have to wash the dishes, or we won't have clean plates for dinner.

4. The yellow flowers are blooming. The red flowers are not.
The yellow flowers are blooming, but the red flowers are not.

5. I like banana cream pie. I like chocolate donuts.
I like banana cream pie, and I like chocolate donuts.

83

"And," "But," "Or"

Directions: Write **and**, **but** or **or** to complete the sentences.

1. I thought we might try that new hamburger place, __but__ Mom wants to eat at the Spaghetti Shop.

2. We could stay home, __or__ would you rather go to the game?

3. She went right home after school, __but__ he stopped at the store.

4. Mother held the piece of paneling, __and__ Father nailed it in place.

5. She babysat last weekend, __and__ her big sister went with her.

6. She likes raisins in her oatmeal, __but__ I would rather have mine with brown sugar.

7. She was planning on coming over tomorrow, __but__ I asked her if she could wait until the weekend.

8. Tomato soup with crackers sounds good to me, __or__ would you rather have vegetable beef soup?

84

"Because" and "So"

Directions: Write **because** or **so** to complete the sentences.

1. She cleaned the paint brushes __so__ they would be ready in the morning.

2. Father called home complaining of a sore throat __so__ Mom stopped by the pharmacy.

3. His bus will be running late __because__ it has a flat tire.

4. We all worked together __so__ we could get the job done sooner.

5. We took a variety of sandwiches on the picnic __because__ we knew not everyone liked cheese and olives with mayonnaise.

6. All the school children were sent home __because__ the electricity went off at school.

7. My brother wants us to meet his girlfriend __so__ she will be coming to dinner with us on Friday.

8. He forgot to take his umbrella along this morning __so__ now his clothes are very wet.

85

"When" and "After"

Directions: Write **when** or **after** to complete the sentences.

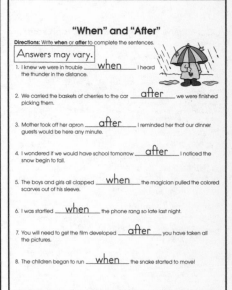

| Answers may vary. |

1. I knew we were in trouble __when__ I heard the thunder in the distance.

2. We carried the baskets of cherries to the car __after__ we were finished picking them.

3. Mother took off her apron __after__ I reminded her that our dinner guests would be here any minute.

4. I wondered if we would have school tomorrow __after__ I noticed the snow begin to fall.

5. The boys and girls all clapped __when__ the magician pulled the colored scarves out of his sleeve.

6. I was startled __when__ the phone rang so late last night.

7. You will need to get the film developed __after__ you have taken all the pictures.

8. The children began to run __when__ the snake started to move!

86

Conjunctions

Directions: Choose the best conjunction from the box to combine the pairs of sentences. Then rewrite the sentences.

| and but or because when after so |

1. I like Leah. I like Ben.
I like Leah and Ben.

2. Should I eat the orange? Should I eat the apple?
Should I eat the orange or the apple?

3. You will get a reward. You turned in the lost item.
You will get a reward because you turned in the lost item.

4. I really mean what I say! You had better listen!
I really mean what I say, and you had better listen!

5. I like you. You're nice, friendly, helpful and kind.
I like you because you're nice, friendly, helpful and kind.

6. You can have dessert. You ate all your peas.
You can have dessert because you ate all your peas.

7. I like your shirt better. You should decide for yourself.
I like your shirt better, but you should decide for yourself.

8. We walked out of the building. We heard the fire alarm.
We walked out of the building after we heard the fire alarm.

9. I like to sing folk songs. I like to play the guitar.
I like to sing folk songs, and I like to play the guitar.

Answers may vary:

87

Run-On Sentences

A **run-on sentence** occurs when two or more sentences are joined together without punctuation.

Examples:

Run-on sentence: I lost my way once did you?
Two sentences with correct punctuation: I lost my way once. Did you?
Run-on sentence: I found the recipe it was not hard to follow.
Two sentences with correct punctuation: I found the recipe. It was not hard to follow.

Directions: Rewrite the run-on sentences correctly with periods, exclamation points and question marks. The first one has been done for you.

1. Did you take my umbrella I can't find it anywhere!
Did you take my umbrella? I can't find it anywhere!

2. How can you stand that noise I can't!
How can you stand that noise? I can't!

3. The cookies are gone I see only crumbs.
The cookies are gone. I see only crumbs.

4. The dogs were barking they were hungry.
The dogs were barking. They were hungry.

5. She is quite ill please call a doctor immediately!
She is quite ill. Please call a doctor immediately!

6. The clouds came up we knew the storm would hit soon.
The clouds came up. We knew the storm would hit soon.

7. You weren't home he stopped by this morning.
You weren't home. He stopped by this morning.

88

Combining Sentences

Some simple sentences can be easily combined into one sentence.

Examples:

Simple sentences: The bird sang. The bird was tiny. The bird was in the tree.
Combined sentence: The tiny bird sang in the tree.

Directions: Combine each set of simple sentences into one sentence. The first one has been done for you.

1. The big girls laughed. They were friendly. They helped the little girls.
The big, friendly girls laughed as they helped the little girls.

2. The dog was hungry. The dog whimpered. The dog looked at its bowl.
_____

3. Be quiet now. I want you to listen. You listen to my joke!
_____

4. I lost my p_____

5. I see my mother. My mother is walking. My mother is walking down the street.
_____

6. Do you like ice cream? Do you like hot dogs? Do you like mustard?
_____

7. Tell me you'll do it! Tell me you will! Tell me right now!
_____

Answers may vary.

89

Combining Sentences in Paragraph Form

A **paragraph** is a group of sentences that share the same idea.

Directions: Rewrite the paragraph by combining the simple sentences into larger sentences.

Jason awoke early. He threw off his covers. He ran to his window. He looked outside. He saw snow. It was white and fluffy. Jason thought of something. He thought of his sled. His sled was in the garage. He quickly ate breakfast. He dressed warmly. He got his sled. He went outside. He went to play in the snow.

Jason awoke early and threw off his covers. He ran to his window and looked outside. He saw white and fluffy snow. Jason thought of his sled in the garage. He quickly ate breakfast and dressed warmly. He got his sled and went outside to play in the snow.

Answer may vary.

90

Review

Directions: Write **S** for statement, **R** for request, **C** for command, **Q** for question or **E** for exclamation.

_R_ 1. Please hand me that tool.
_C_ 2. Give me that hammer.
_E_ 3. That hurts!
_S_ 4. The class meets at noon today.
_Q_ 5. Will you be at the meeting?
_C_ 6. Open your fingers wide.

Directions: Rewrite these sentences as questions.

7. Please come here. _Would you please come here?_
8. He wondered where we were. _Did he wonder where we were?_

Directions: Rewrite these run-on sentences correctly with periods, exclamation marks or question marks.

9. I won't bother you I'll just wait. _I won't bother you. I'll just wait._
10. Trust me I'm a true friend. _Trust me. I'm a true friend._

Directions: Combine and rewrite these sets of simple sentences. *Answers may vary.*

11. The baby was cheerful. The baby was smiling. The baby was a joy to be around.
The baby was cheerful, smiling and a joy to be around.

12. I lost my hammer. I lost my nails. I lost my patience.
I lost my hammer, my nails and my patience.

Directions: Use conjunctions to combine these sentences. *Answers may vary.*

13. I like ripe bananas. He likes green bananas.
I like ripe bananas, and he likes green bananas.

14. I will add up the charges. I will tell you the costs.
I will add up the charges and tell you the costs.

91

Punctuation: Commas

Use a comma to separate the number of the day of a month and the year. Do not use a comma to separate the month and year if no day is given.

Examples:

June 14, 1999
June 1999

Use a comma after **yes** or **no** when it is the first word in a sentence.

Examples:

Yes, I will do it right now.
No, I don't want any.

Directions: Write **C** if the sentence is punctuated correctly. Draw an **X** if the sentence is not punctuated correctly. The first one has been done for you.

_C_ 1. No. I don't plan to attend.
_C_ 2. I told them, oh yes, I would go.
_C_ 3. Her birthday is March 13, 1995.
_X_ 4. He was born in May, 1997.
_C_ 5. Yes, of course I like you!
_X_ 6. No I will not be there.
_X_ 7. They left for vacation on February, 14.
_C_ 8. No, today is Monday.
_C_ 9. The program was first shown on August 12, 1991.
_X_ 10. In September, 2007 how old will you be?
_X_ 11. He turned 12 years old on November, 13.
_X_ 12. I said no, I will not come no matter what!
_C_ 13. Yes, she is a friend of mine.
_C_ 14. His birthday is June 12, 1992, and mine is June 12, 1993.
_X_ 15. No I would not like more dessert.

92

Punctuation: Commas

Use a comma to separate words in a series. A comma is used after each word in a series but is not needed before the last word. Both ways are correct. In your own writing, be consistent about which style you use.

Examples:

We ate apples, oranges, and pears.
We ate apples, oranges and pears.

Always use a comma between the name of a city and a state.

Example:

She lives in Fresno, California.
He lives in Wilmington, Delaware.

Directions: Write **C** if the sentence is punctuated correctly. Draw an **X** if the sentence is not punctuated correctly. The first one has been done for you.

X 1. She ordered shoes, dresses and shirts to be sent to her home in Oakland California.
C 2. No one knew her pets' names were Fido, Spot and Tiger.
X 3. He likes green beans lima beans, and corn on the cob.
C 4. Typing paper, pens and pencils are all needed for school.
C 5. Send your letters to her in College Park, Maryland.
X 6. Orlando Florida is the home of Disney World.
C 7. Mickey, Minnie, Goofy and Daisy are all favorites of mine.
C 8. Send your letter to her in Reno, Nevada.
X 9. Before he lived in New York, City he lived in San Diego, California.
C 10. She mailed postcards, and letters to him in Lexington, Kentucky.
C 11. Teacups, saucers, napkins, and silverware were piled high.
C 12. Can someone give me a ride to Indianapolis, Indiana?
C 13. He took a train a car, then a boat to visit his old friend.
X 14. Why can't I go to Disney World to see Mickey, and Minnie?

93

Punctuation: Quotation Marks

Use quotation marks (" ") before and after the exact words of a speaker.

Examples:

I asked Aunt Martha, "How do you feel?"
"I feel awful," Aunt Martha replied.

Do not put quotation marks around words that report what the speaker said.

Examples:

Aunt Martha said she felt awful.
I asked Aunt Martha how she felt.

Directions: Write **C** if the sentence is punctuated correctly. Draw an **X** if the sentence is not punctuated correctly. The first one has been done for you.

C 1. "I want it right now!" she demanded angrily.
X 2. "Do you want it now? I asked.
X 3. She said "she felt better" now.
C 4. Her exact words were, "I feel much better now!"
C 5. "I am so thrilled to be here!" he shouted.
X 6. "Yes, I will attend," she replied.
X 7. Elizabeth said "she was unhappy."
C 8. "I'm unhappy," Elizabeth reported.
C 9. "Did you know her mother?" I asked.
X 10. I asked "whether you knew her mother."
C 11. I wondered, "What will dessert be?"
C 12. "Which will it be, salt or pepper?" the waiter asked.
C 13. "No, I don't know the answer!" he snapped.
X 14. He said "yes he'd take her on the trip."
X 15. Be patient, he said. "It will soon be over."

94

Punctuation: Quotation Marks

Use quotation marks around the titles of songs and poems.

Examples:

Have you heard "Still Cruising" by the Beach Boys?
"Ode To a Nightingale" is a famous poem.

Directions: Write **C** if the sentence is punctuated correctly. Draw an **X** if the sentence is not punctuated correctly. The first one has been done for you.

C 1. Do you know "My Bonnie Lies Over the Ocean"?
X 2. We sang The Stars and Stripes Forever" at school.
C 3. Her favorite song is "The Eensy Weensy Spider."
X 4. Turn the music up when "A Hard Day's "Night comes on!
C 5. "Yesterday" was one of Paul McCartney's most famous songs.
C 6. "Mary Had a Little Lamb" is a very silly poem!
C 7. A song everyone knows is "Happy Birthday."
X 8. "Swing Low, Sweet Chariot" was first sung by slaves.
X 9. Do you know the words to Home on "the Range"?
C 10. "Hiawatha" is a poem many older people had to memorize.
X 11. "Happy Days Are Here Again! is an upbeat tune.
C 12. Frankie Valli and the Four Seasons sang "Sherry."
X 13. The words to "Rain, Rain" Go Away are easy to learn.
C 14. A slow song I know is called "Summertime."
C 15. Little children like to hear "The Night Before Christmas."

95

Book Titles

All words in the title of a book are underlined. Underlined words also mean italics.

Examples:

The Hunt for Red October was a best-seller!
(The Hunt for Red October)
Have you read Lost in Space? (Lost in Space)

Directions: Underline the book titles in these sentences. The first one has been done for you.

1. The Dinosaur Poster Book is for eight year olds.
2. Have you read Lion Dancer by Kate Waters?
3. Baby Dinosaurs and Giant Dinosaurs were both written by Peter Dodson.
4. Have you heard of the book That's What Friends Are For by Carol Adorjan?
5. J.B. Stamper wrote a book called The Totally Terrific Valentine Party Book.
6. The teacher read Almost Ten and a Half aloud to our class.
7. Marrying Off Mom is about a girl who tries to get her widowed mother to start dating.
8. The Snow and The Fire are the second and third books by author Caroline Cooney.
9. The title sounds silly, but Goofbang Value Daze really is the name of a book!
10. A book about space exploration is The Day We Walked on the Moon by George Sullivan.
11. Alice and the Birthday Giant tells about a giant who came to a girl's birthday party.
12. A book about a girl who is sad about her father's death is called Rachel and the Upside Down Heart by Eileen Douglas.
13. Two books about baseball are Baseball Bloopers and Oddball Baseball.
14. Katharine Ross wrote Teenage Mutant Ninja Turtles: The Movie Storybook.

96

Book Titles

Capitalize the first and last word of book titles. Capitalize all other words of book titles except short prepositions, such as **of**, **at** and **in**; conjunctions, such as **and**, **or** and **but**; and articles, such as **a**, **an** and **the**.

Examples:

Have you read War and Peace?
Pippi Longstocking in Moscow is her favorite book.

Directions: Underline the book titles. Circle the words that should be capitalized. The first one has been done for you.

1. murder in the blue room by Elliot Roosevelt
2. growing up in a divided society by Sandra Burnham
3. the corn king and the spring queen by Naomi Mitchison
4. new kids on the block by Grace Catalano
5. best friends don't tell lies by Linda Barr
6. turn your kid into a computer genius by Carole Gerber
7. 50 simple things you can do to save the earth by Earth Works Press
8. garfield goes to waist by Jim Davis
9. the hunt for red october by Tom Clancy
10. fall into darkness by Christopher Pike
11. oh the places you'll go! by Dr. Seuss
12. amy the dancing bear by Carly Simon
13. the great waldo search by Martin Handford
14. the time and space of uncle albert by Russel Stannard
15. true stories about abraham lincoln by Ruth Gross

97

Capital Letters and Periods

The first letter of a person's first, last and middle name is always capitalized.

Example: Elizabeth Jane Marks is my best friend.

The first letter of a person's title is always capitalized. If the title is abbreviated, the title is followed by a period.

Examples: Her mother is Dr. Susan Jones Marks.
Ms. Jessica Joseph was a visitor.

C if the sentence is punctuated and capitalized correctly. Draw an **X** if the sentence is not punctuated and capitalized correctly. The first one has been done for you.

X 1. I asked Elizabeth if I should call her mother Mrs. marks or dr. Marks.
C 2. Mr. and Mrs. Francesco were friends of the DeVuonos.
X 3. Dr. Daniel Long and Dr Holly Barrows both spoke with the patient.
C 4. Did you get Mr. MacMillan for English next year?
C 5. Mr. Sweet and Ms. Ellison were both at the concert.
X 6. When did the doctor. tell you about this illness?
C 7. Dr. Donovan is the doctor that Mr. Winham trusted.
C 8. Why don't you ask Doctor. Williams her opinion?
X 9. All three of the doctors diagnosed Ms. Twelp.
X 10. Will Ms. Davis and Ms Simpson be at school today?
X 11. Did Dr Samuels see your father last week?
C 12. Is Judy a medical doctor or another kind of specialist?
X 13. We are pleased to introduce Ms King and Mr. Graham.

98

ENGLISH 4

Review

Directions: The following sentences have errors in punctuation, capitalization or both. The number in parentheses **( )** at the end of each sentence tells you how many errors it contains. Correct the errors by rewriting each sentence.

1. I saw mr. Johnson reading War And Peace to his class. (2)

I saw Mr. Johnson reading War and Peace to his class.

2. Do you like to sing "Take me Out to The Ballgame"? (2)

Do you like to sing "Take Me Out to the Ballgame"?

3. He recited Hiawatha to Miss. Simpson's class. (2)

He recited Hiawatha to Miss Simpson's class.

4. Bananas, and oranges are among Dr smith's favorite fruits. (3)

Bananas and oranges are among Dr. Smith's favorite fruits.

5. "Daisy, daisy is a song about a bicycle built for two. (2)

"Daisy, Daisy" is a song about a bicycle built for two.

6. Good Morning, Granny Rose is about a woman and her dog. (1)

"Good Morning, Granny Rose" is about a woman and her dog.

7. Garfield goes to waist is a very funny book! (3)

Garfield Goes to Waist is a very funny book!

8. Peanut butter, jelly, and bread are Miss. Lee's favorite treats. (1)

Peanut butter, jelly and bread are Miss Lee's favorite treats.

99

Proofreading

Proofreading means searching for and correcting errors by carefully reading and rereading what has been written. Use the proofreading marks below when correcting your writing or someone else's.

To insert a word or a punctuation mark that has been left out, use this mark: ∧. It is called a caret.
Example: We˄to the dance together.

To show that a letter should be capitalized, put three lines under it.
Example: Mrs. jones drove us to school.

To show that a capital letter should be a small or lower-case, draw a diagonal line through it.
Example: Mrs. Jones Drove us to school.

To show that a word is spelled incorrectly, draw a horizontal line through it and write the correct spelling above it.
Example: The wolros is an amazing animal.

Directions: Proofread the two paragraphs using the proofreading marks you learned. The author's last name, Towne, is spelled correctly.

The Modern ark

My book report is on the modern ark by Cecilia Fitzsimmons. The book tells abut 80 of the worlds endangered animals. The book also an arc and animals inside for kids put together.

Their House

More house is a Great book! The arthur's name is Mary Towne. they're house tells about a girl name Molly. Molly's Family bys an old house from some people named warren. Then there big problems begin!

100

Proofreading

Directions: Proofread the paragraphs, using the proofreading marks you learned. There are seven capitalization errors, three missing words and eleven errors in spelling or word usage.

Key West

key West has been tropical paradise ever since Ponce de Leon first saw the set of islands called the keys in 1513. Two famus streets in Key West are named duval and whitehead. You will find the city cemetery on Francis Street. The tombstones are funny!

The message on one is, "I told you I was sick!" On sailor's tombston is this mesage his widow: "At least I no where to find him now."

The cemetery is on 21 acres in the middle of town.

The most famous home in key west is that of the author, Ernest Hemingway. Hemingway's home was at 907 whitehead Street. He lived their for 30 years.

101

Proofreading

Directions: Read more about Key West. Proofread and correct the errors. There are eight errors in capitalization, seven misspelled words, a missing comma and three missing words.

More About Key West

a good way to lurn more about key West is to ride the trolley. Key West has a great trolly system. The trolley will take on a tour of the salt ponds. You can also three red brick forts. The trolley tour goes by a 110-foot high lighthouse. It is rite in the middle of the city. Key west is the only city with a lighthouse in the middle of it! It is also the southernmost city in the United States.

If you have time, the new Ship Wreck Museum. Key west was also the hom of former president Harry truman. During his presidency, Truman spent many vacations on key west.

102

Proofreading

Directions: Proofread the sentences. Write **C** if the sentence has no errors. Draw an **X** if the sentence contains missing words or other errors. The first one has been done for you.

C 1. The new Ship Wreck Museum in Key West is exciting!

X 2. Another thing I liked was the litehouse.

C 3. Do you remember Hemingway's address in Key West?

X 4. The Key West semetery is on 21 acres of ground.

X 5. Ponce de eon discovered Key West.

C 6. The cemetery in Key West is on Francis Street.

X 7. My favorete tombstone was the sailor's.

C 8. His wife wrote the words on it. Remember?

X 9. The words said, "at least I know where to find him now!"

C 10. That sailor must have been away at sea all the time.

X 11. The troley ride around Key West is very interesting.

X 12. Do you why it is called Key West?

C 13. Can you imagine a lighthouse in the middle of your town?

X 14. It's interesting to no that Key West is our southernmost city.

C 15. Besides Harry Truman and Hemingway, did other famous people live there?

103

Proofreading

Directions: Each of the following sentences has a word missing. Use a caret to insert the missing word. The first one has been done for you.

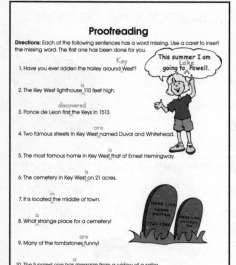

This summer I am going to Powell.
Lake

Key
1. Have you ever ridden the trolley around ⌄West?

is
2. The Key West lighthouse ⌄110 feet high.

discovered
3. Ponce de Leon first ⌄the Keys in 1513.

are
4. Two famous streets in Key West ⌄named Duval and Whitehead.

is
5. The most famous home in Key West ⌄that of Ernest Hemingway.

is
6. The cemetery in Key West ⌄on 21 acres.

in
7. It is located ⌄the middle of town.

a
8. What strange place for a cemetery!

are
9. Many of the tombstones ⌄funny!

a
10. The funniest one has ⌄message from a widow of a sailor.

Review

Directions: Use the correct proofreading marks to show the two capitalization errors in each sentence.

1. Mrs. edwards drove us to edison Elementary School.

2. Who can say what john's real problem was?

3. Did you tell dr. Lynn we would be there at noon?

4. My Aunt Nellie was there and so was aunt susan.

Directions: Use the correct proofreading mark to insert the missing word or letter in each sentence.

'd
5. He promised me he⌄be there on time!

can
6. Who⌄tell me the answer to the first problem?

was
7. What his nickname when he was a baby?

the
8. Did he tell you⌄same thing?

Directions: Use the correct proofreading mark, then correct the misspelled or misused word in each sentence.

principal
9. I wondered if the prineepal knew what had happened.

heard
10. I herd her whole family was there!

easily
11. Our team easley beat the other team.

too
12. Don't laugh te hard at those silly jokes!

104   105

Teaching Suggestions

Subjects and Predicates

Have your child dictate five to ten sentences to you. Write them on strips of paper. Cut the strips between the subject and the predicate. Mix up the subject sections and place them in one pile. Place the predicate sections in another pile. Have your child put the sentences back together so they make sense. **Example:** He / caught the ball and ran for a touchdown.

Your child can use these sentence strips and make new subjects for the predicates and new predicates for the subjects. **Example:** The running back /caught the ball and ran for a touchdown.

Make "silly sentences" with your child by combining a subject and a predicate that usually don't belong together. Have your child glue the silly sentence to a piece of drawing paper and illustrate it. **Example:** The cuddly kitten / caught the ball and ran for a touchdown.

Identifying Parts of Speech

Help your child learn or review parts of a sentence using a dictionary. Explain that a dictionary entry is a reference that will help identify parts of speech. Examine several dictionary entries together. When your child has difficulty recognizing what part of speech a word is, the dictionary can be a ready source.

Nouns and Adjectives

Remind your child that a noun names a person, place or thing. Have children write nouns on plain white index cards. Remind your child that an adjective describes a noun. Have him/her write adjectives on colored index cards. Since adjectives are describing words, this can visually help your child connect adjectives with ways to make sentences more colorful. He/she could match the cards to show nouns and adjectives that would go together.

Practice recognizing adjectives and nouns when you and your child are in the car on a trip or waiting at a traffic light. Point out an object or a building. Ask your child to name adjectives to describe it. Challenge your child to come up with 10 describing words in a specified length of time.

Adverbs

Adverbs tell place, time or manner. Have your child label three containers with those words. One container could be decorated to represent a building (place), one to represent a clock (time) and one with a big smiley face (manner). Give your child adverb word cards and have him/her put them in the right container. He/she could select an adverb and write a sentence using that word.

Using Words Correctly

On index cards or poster board pieces, write the following words: **good**, **well**, **your**, **you're**, **its**, **it's**, **can**, **may**, **sit**, **set**, **they're**, **their**, **there**, **this** and **these**.

On additional pieces, write sentences that have one of the above words missing. After shuffling the word cards and the sentence cards, place them facedown on two separate areas. Have the first player turn over a word card and a sentence card and see if they match. If they do, the player keeps the match and takes another turn. If there is no match, turn the cards facedown and the next player selects two cards. Play continues until all the cards have been matched.

Capitalization

Help your child write a letter to a relative or friend. Remind him or her that proper nouns begin with capital letters. Check the return address and the mailing address to make sure capital letters are used where needed. You may want your child to practice addressing an envelope on a sheet of paper before writing on an envelope.

Help your child develop listening skills while playing a capitalization game. Have your child listen as you say a sentence. Have him/her say which word or words need to be capitalized and why those words should begin with a capital letter.

Your child can list the days of the week or months of the year, write down names of family members, stores in your community or names of the streets in your neighborhood. This will provide good practice in writing proper nouns with capital letters.

Proofreading

As your child writes sentences and stories, he/she needs to be able to express his/her thoughts without concern for correct spelling and punctuation. The first draft of a story should be one in which the writer doesn't worry about mechanics. He/she needs to get his/her thoughts down. When the story is completed, you can guide your child in proofreading before making a final copy.

Proofreading should consist of looking for grammatical errors, overuse of words (synonyms could be used instead), misspellings, punctuation mistakes and capitalization errors. Work with your child without being critical to enable him/her to see the types of mistakes he/she made. Make the corrections together until you see that your child is able to handle proofreading on his/her own.

You could do some practice sentences, providing written work with obvious mistakes and have your child correct them. The mistakes, at first, could be names of family members or pets. Help your child rewrite them with the corrections made. You may want to write sentences with blank spaces and have your child write the missing proper nouns. Progress to other types of errors such as commas, quotation marks, question marks and misspelled words.